P9-CDG-707

❧ Michael Hague's ❧
Family Easter Treasury

HENRY HOLT AND COMPANY
New York

Henry Holt and Company, Inc., *Publishers since 1866,*
115 West 18th Street. New York, New York 10011

Henry Holt is a registered trademark of Henry Holt and Company, Inc.

Compilation copyright © 1999 by Henry Holt and Company, Inc.
Illustrations copyright © 1999 by Michael Hague. All rights reserved.
Published in Canada by Fitzhenry & Whiteside Ltd.,
195 Allstate Parkway, Markham, Ontario L3R 4T8.

Library of Congress Cataloging-in-Publication Data
Michael Hague's family Easter treasury.
 p. cm.
Summary: An anthology of thirty-two stories, sacred texts, and poems that celebrate Easter.
1. Easter–Literary collections. [1. Easter–Literary collections] I. Hague, Michael.
 PZ5.M588635 1999 808.8'033–dc20 95-46916

ISBN 0-8050-3819-1/First Edition–1999
Printed in Italy
The artist used mixed media on watercolor board to create the illustrations for this book.
 1 3 5 7 9 10 8 6 4 2

Permission for the use of the following is gratefully acknowledged:

"Sing, All Ye Christian People!" by Jan Struther. Copyright © 1931, from *Enlarged Songs of Praise;*
 used by permission of Oxford University Press.

"Spring Song" copyright © 1987 by Lucille Clifton. Reprinted from *Good Women: Poems and a
 Memoir, 1969-1980,* by Lucille Clifton, with permission of BOA Editions, Ltd, 92 Park Ave.,
 Brockport, NY 14420.

"Easter's Coming" copyright © 1967 by Aileen Fisher. Used by permission of the author, Aileen
 Fisher, who controls rights.

"The Easter Parade" from *Laughing Time: Collected Nonsense* by William Jay Smith. Copyright © 1990
 by William Jay Smith. Reprinted by permission of Farrar, Straus & Giroux, Inc.

"Easter: For Penny" from *Celebrations* by Myra Cohn Livingston (Holiday House). Copyright
 © 1985 by Myra Cohn Livingston. Reprinted by permission of Marion Reiner for the author.

"Bramble and Buckwheat" copyright © 1997 by Ethel Pochocki. Printed courtesy of the author.

"The White Blackbird" reprinted with the permission of Simon & Schuster Books for Young
 Readers from *The Peep-Show Man* by Padraic Colum. Copyright 1924 by Macmillan Publishing
 Company; copyright renewed 1952 by Padraic Colum.

"The Easter Flower" copyright © 1953 by Claude McKay. Used by permission of the Archives of
 Claude McKay, Carl Cowl, administrator.

"The Sun Comes Dancing" reprinted with the permission of Simon & Schuster Books for Young
 Readers from *Twelve Months Make a Year* by Elizabeth Coatsworth. Copyright 1943 by
 Macmillan Publishing Company; copyright renewed © 1971 by Elizabeth Coatsworth Beston.

Every effort has been made to trace copyright holders. Henry Holt and Company Books
 for Young Readers would be interested to hear from any copyright holders not here
 acknowledged.

To the memory of Gordon Saul
—M. H.

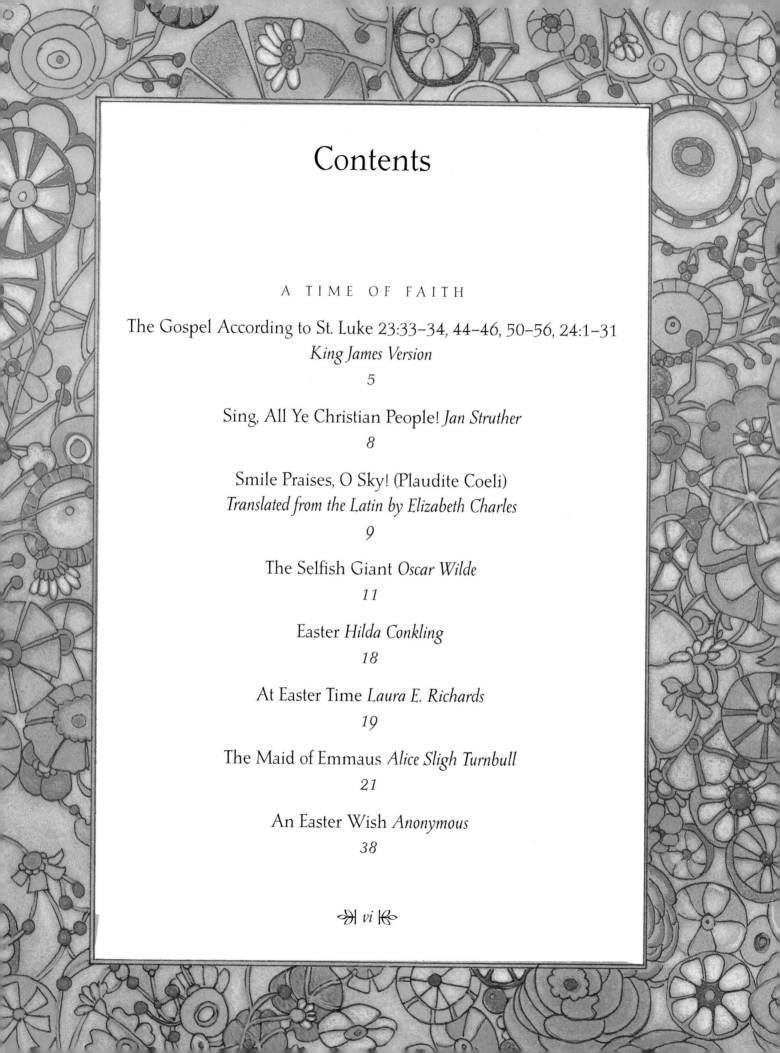

Contents

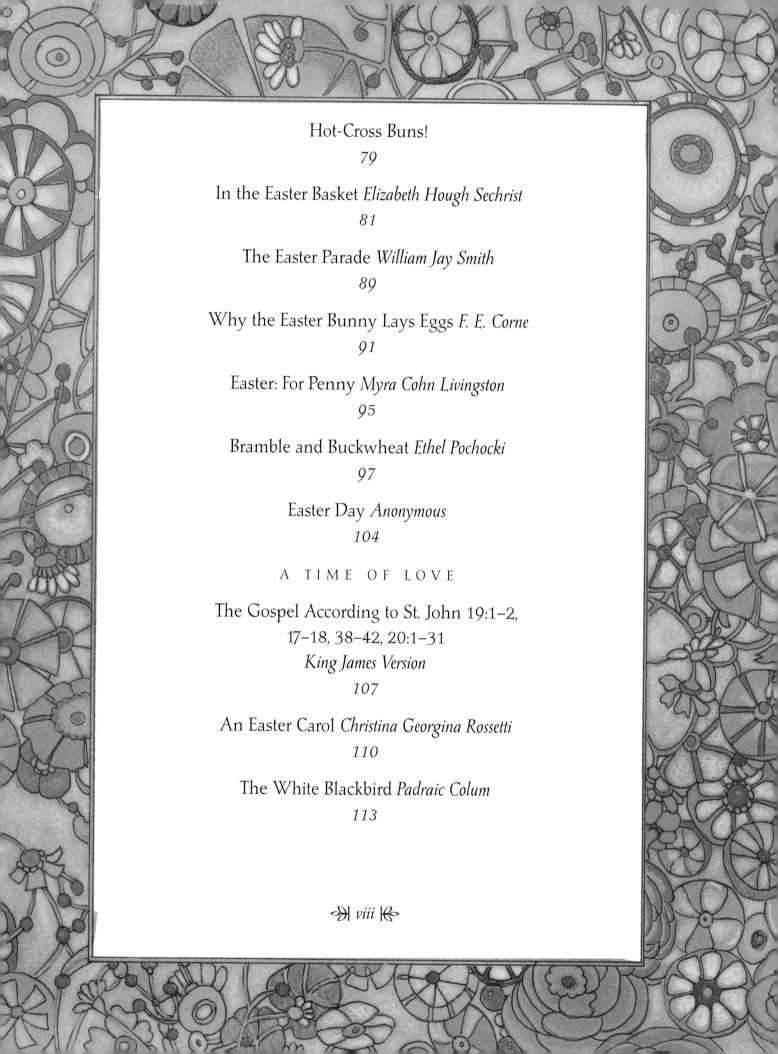

A TIME OF LOVE

Michael Hague's
Family Easter Treasury

A Time of Faith

The Gospel According to St. Luke
23:33–34, 44–46, 50–56, 24:1–31

KING JAMES VERSION

And when they were come to the place, which is called Calvary, there they crucified him, and the malefactors, one on the right hand, and the other on the left. Then said Jesus, Father, forgive them; for they know not what they do. And they parted his raiment, and cast lots.

And it was about the sixth hour, and there was a darkness over all the earth until the ninth hour. And the sun was darkened, and the veil of the temple was rent in the midst. And when Jesus had cried with a loud voice, he said, Father, into thy hands I commend my spirit: and having said thus, he gave up the ghost.

And, behold, there was a man named Joseph, a counseller; and he was a good man, and a just: (The same had not consented to the counsel and deed of them;) he was of Arimathaea, a city of the Jews: who also himself waited for the kingdom of God. This man went unto Pilate, and begged the body of Jesus. And he took it down, and wrapped it in linen, and laid it in a sepulchre that was hewn in stone, wherein never man before was laid. And that day was the preparation, and the sabbath drew on. And the women also, which came with him from Galilee, followed after, and beheld the sepulchre, and how his body was laid. And they returned, and prepared spices and ointments; and rested the sabbath day according to the commandment.

Now upon the first day of the week, very early in the morning, they came unto the sepulchre, bringing the spices which they had prepared, and certain others with them. And they found the stone rolled away from the sepulchre. And they entered in, and found not the body of the Lord Jesus. And it came to pass, as they were much perplexed thereabout, behold, two men stood by them in shining garments: And as they were afraid, and bowed down their faces to the earth, they said unto them, Why seek ye the living among the dead? He is not here, but is risen: remember how he spake unto you when he was yet in Galilee, saying, The Son of man must be delivered into the hands of sinful men, and be crucified, and the third day rise again. And they remembered his words. And returned from the sepulchre, and told all these things unto the eleven, and to all the rest.

It was Mary Magdalene, and Joanna, and Mary the mother of James, and other women that were with them, which told these things unto the apostles. And their words seemed to them as idle tales, and they believed them not. Then arose Peter, and ran unto the sepulchre; and stooping down, he beheld the linen clothes laid by themselves, and departed, wondering in himself at that which was come to pass. And, behold, two of them went that same day to a village called Emmaus, which was from Jerusalem about threescore furlongs. And they talked together of all these things which had happened. And it came to pass, that, while they communed together and reasoned, Jesus himself drew near, and went with them. But their eyes were holden that they should not know him. And he said unto them, What manner of communications are these that ye have one to another, as ye walk, and are sad? And the one of them, whose name was Cleopas, answering said unto him, Art thou only a stranger in Jerusalem, and hast not known the things which are come to pass therein these days? And he said unto them, What things? And they said unto him, Concerning

Jesus of Nazareth, which was a prophet mighty in deed and word before God and all the people: And how the chief priests and our rulers delivered him to be condemned to death, and have crucified him. But we trusted that it had been he which should have redeemed Israel: and beside all this, to day is the third day since these things were done. Yea, and certain women also of our company made us astonished, which were early at the sepulchre; And when they found not his body, they came, saying, that they had also seen a vision of angels, which said that he was alive. And certain of them which were with us went to the sepulchre, and found it even so as the women had said: but him they saw not. Then he said unto them, O fools, and slow of heart to believe all that the prophets have spoken: Ought not Christ to have suffered these things, and to enter into his glory? And beginning at Moses and all the prophets, he expounded unto them in all the scriptures the things concerning himself. And they drew nigh unto the village, whither they went: and he made as though he would have gone further. But they constrained him, saying, Abide with us: for it is toward evening, and the day is far spent. And he went in to tarry with them. And it came to pass, as he sat at meat with them, he took bread, and blessed it, and brake, and gave to them. And their eyes were opened, and they knew him; and he vanished out of their sight.

Sing,
All Ye Christian People!

JAN STRUTHER

Sing, all ye Christian people!
Swing, bells, in every steeple!
  For Christ to life is risen,
  Set free from death's dark prison.
With joyfulness, with joyfulness your
  alleluyas sing,
For Christ has come again to greet the spring.

Green now is on the larches;
Springtime in triumph marches,
  And every day uncloses
  A host of new primroses:
Then daffodils and marybuds
  let us in garlands bring,
For Christ has come again to greet the spring.

Skylarks, the earth forsaking,
Soar to their music-making,
  And in the roof-tree's hollow
  Now builds the trusting swallow:
So cries to him, so flies to him
  my soul on fearless wing,
For Christ has come again to greet the spring.

Smile Praises, O Sky!

(PLAUDITE COELI)

Translated from the Latin by Elizabeth Charles

Smile praises, O sky!
  Soft breathe them, O air!
Below and on high,
  And everywhere.
The black troop of storms
  Has yielded to calm;
Tufted blossoms are peeping,
And early palm.

Arouse thee, O spring!
  Ye flowers, come forth,
With thousand hues tinting
  The soft green earth;
Ye violets tender,
  And sweet roses bright,
Gay Lent-lilies blended
  With pure lilies white.

The Selfish Giant

O S C A R   W I L D E

Every afternoon, as they were coming from school, the children used to go and play in the Giant's garden.

It was a large lovely garden, with soft green grass. Here and there over the grass stood beautiful flowers like stars, and there were twelve peach-trees that in the spring-time broke out into delicate blossoms of pink and pearl, and in the autumn bore rich fruit. The birds sat on the trees and sang so sweetly that the children used to stop their games in order to listen to them. "How happy we are here!" they cried to each other.

One day the Giant came back. He had been to visit his friend the Cornish ogre, and had stayed with him for seven years. After the seven years were over he had said all that he had to say, for his conversation was limited, and he determined to return to his own castle. When he arrived he saw the children playing in the garden.

"What are you doing here?" he cried in a very gruff voice, and the children ran away.

"My own garden is my own garden," said the Giant; "anyone can understand that, and I will allow nobody to play in it but myself." So he built a high wall all round it, and put up a notice-board.

TRESPASSERS
will be
PROSECUTED

He was a very selfish Giant.
The poor children had now nowhere to play. They tried to play

on the road, but the road was very dusty and full of hard stones, and they did not like it. They used to wander round the high walls when their lessons were over, and talk about the beautiful garden inside. "How happy we were there!" they said to each other.

Then the Spring came, and all over the country there were little blossoms and little birds. Only in the garden of the Selfish Giant it was still winter. The birds did not care to sing in it as there were no children, and the trees forgot to blossom. Once a beautiful flower put its head out from the grass, but when it saw the notice-board it was so sorry for the children that it slipped back into the ground again, and went off to sleep. The only people who were pleased were the Snow and the Frost. "Spring has forgotten this garden," they cried, "so we will live here all the year round." The Snow covered up the grass with her great white cloak, and the Frost painted all the trees silver. Then they invited the North Wind to stay with them, and he came. He was wrapped in furs, and he roared all day about the garden, and blew the chimney-pots down. "This is a delightful spot" he said, "we must ask the Hail on a visit." So the Hail came. Every day for three hours he rattled on the roof of the castle till he broke most of the slates, and then he ran round and round the garden as fast as he could go. He was dressed in gray, and his breath was like ice.

"I cannot understand why the Spring is so late in coming," said the Selfish Giant, as he sat at the window and looked out at his cold, white garden; "I hope there will be a change in the weather."

But the Spring never came, nor the Summer. The Autumn gave golden fruit to every garden, but to the Giant's garden she gave none. "He is too selfish," she said. So it was always winter there, and the North Wind and the Hail, and the Frost, and the Snow danced about through the trees.

One morning the Giant was lying awake in bed when he heard some lovely music. It sounded so sweet to his ears that he thought it must be the King's musicians passing by. It was really only a little linnet singing outside his window, but it was so long since he had heard a bird sing in his garden that it seemed to him to be the most beautiful music in the world. Then the Hail stopped dancing over his head, and the North Wind ceased roaring, and a delicious perfume came to him through the open casement. "I believe the Spring has come at last," said the Giant; and he jumped out of bed and looked out.

What did he see?

He saw a most wonderful sight. Through a little hole in the wall the children had crept in, and they were sitting in the branches of the trees. In every tree that he could see there was a little child. And the trees were so glad to have the children back again that they had covered themselves with blossoms, and were waving their arms gently above the children's heads. The birds were flying about and twittering with delight, and the flowers were looking up through the green grass and laughing. It was a lovely scene, only in one corner it was still winter. It was the farthest corner of the garden, and in it was standing a little boy. He was so small that he could not reach up to the branches of the tree, and he was wandering all round it, crying bitterly. The poor tree was still covered with frost and snow, and the North Wind was blowing and roaring above it. "Climb up! little boy," said the Tree, and it bent its branches down as low as it could; but the boy was too tiny.

And the Giant's heart melted as he looked out. "How selfish I have been!" he said: "now I know why the Spring would not come here. I will put that poor little boy on the top of the tree, and then I will knock down the wall, and my garden shall be the children's

playground for ever and ever." He was really very sorry for what he had done.

So he crept downstairs and opened the front door quite softly, and went out into the garden. But when the children saw him they were so frightened that they all ran away, and the garden became winter again. Only the little boy did not run for his eyes were so full of tears that he did not see the Giant coming. And the Giant stole up behind him and took him gently in his hand, and put him up into the tree. And the tree broke at once into blossom, and the birds came and sang on it, and the little boy stretched out his two arms and flung them round the Giant's neck, and kissed him. And the other children when they saw the Giant was not wicked any longer, came running back, and with them came the Spring. "It is your garden now, little children," said the Giant, and he took a great axe and knocked down the wall. And when the people were going to market at twelve o'clock they found the Giant playing with the children in the most beautiful garden they had ever seen.

All day long they played, and in the evening they came to the Giant to bid him good-bye.

"But where is your little companion?" he said: "the boy I put into the tree." The Giant loved him the best because he had kissed him.

"We don't know," answered the children: "he has gone away."

"You must tell him to be sure and come tomorrow," said the Giant. But the children said that they did not know where he lived and had never seen him before; and the Giant felt very sad.

Every afternoon, when school was over, the childrn came and played with the Giant. But the little boy whom the Giant loved was never seen again. The Giant was very kind to all the children, yet he longed for his first little friend, and often spoke of him. "How I would like to see him!" he used to say.

Years went over, and the Giant grew very old and feeble. He could not play about any more, so he sat in a huge armchair, and watched the children at their games, and admired his garden. "I have many beautiful flowers," he said; "but the children are the most beautiful flowers of all."

One winter morning he looked out of his window as he was dressing. He did not hate the Winter now, for he knew that it was merely the Spring asleep, and that the flowers were resting.

Suddenly he rubbed his eyes in wonder and looked and looked. It certainly was a marvellous sight. In the farthest corner of the garden was a tree quite covered with lovely white blossoms. Its branches were golden, and silver fruit hung down from them, and underneath it stood the little boy he had loved.

Downstairs ran the Giant in great joy, and out into the garden.

He hastened across the grass, and came near to the child. And when he came quite close his face grew red with anger, and he said, "Who hath dared to wound thee?" For on the palms of the child's hands were the prints of two nails, and the prints of two nails were on the little feet.

"Who hath dared to wound thee?" cried the Giant, "tell me, that I may take my big sword and slay him."

"Nay," answered the child: "but these are the wounds of Love."

"Who art thou?" said the Giant, and a strange awe fell on him,

and he knelt before the little child.

And the child smiled on the Giant, and said to him, "You let me play once in your garden, today you shall come with me to my garden, which is Paradise."

And when the children ran in that afternoon, they found the Giant lying dead under the tree, all covered with white blossoms.

Easter

HILDA CONKLING

On Easter morn
Up the faint cloudy sky
I hear the Easter bell,
    Ding dong . . . ding dong . . .
Easter morning scatters lilies
On every doorstep;
Easter morning says a glad thing
Over and over.
Poor people, beggars, old women
Are hearing the Easter bell . . .
    Ding dong . . . ding dong . . .

At Easter Time

LAURA E. RICHARDS

The little flowers came through the ground,
  At Easter time, at Easter time;
They raised their heads and looked around,
  A happy Easter time.
And every pretty bud did say,
  "Good people, bless this holy day,
For Christ is risen, the angels say
  At happy Easter time!"

The scarlet lily raised its cup
  At Easter time, at Easter time;
The crocus to the sky looked up
  At happy Easter time.

"We'll hear the song of Heaven!" they say,
  "Its glory shines on us today.
Oh, may it shine on us always
  At holy Easter time!"

'Twas long and long and long ago,
  That Easter time, that Easter time;
But still the scarlet lilies blow,
  At happy Easter time.
And still each little flower doth say
  "Good Christians, bless this holy day,
For Christ is risen, the angels say
At blessed Easter time!"

The Maid of Emmaus

ALICE SLIGH TURNBULL

Passover week, and a long, hard day at the inn in Emmaus! From early morning Martha had run here and there, carrying water from the spring, bringing sticks, washing the wooden bowls, sweeping under the long, bench-like table around which the guests ate, grinding more wheat and barley in the mill by the back doorway, hurrying faster and faster, under the sharp commands from old Sarah and the quick blows from Jonas, the husband of Sarah.

Passover week was always busy. First there came the caravans from the north and west. These found it convenient to stop at the inn for refreshment before they began the last hilly climb which led to Mount Zion itself. Even as the week wore on there were still many travellers, coming singly and in groups, on foot and on donkeys, but going, going, always going toward Jerusalem. When the Sabbath was past they would all begin to come back, and then there would be another busy time at the inn.

But this week, in spite of the hard days and the blows that seemed somehow to grow more numerous as business increased, Martha had moved as if in a happy dream. She had scarcely seen the faces of the strangers as they sat about the table or passed by on the street; she had obeyed endless harsh directions and surly shouts quickly and mechanically, but with a look that was far away; she had heard never a word of the gossip or comment in the long inn room or around the doorway; for she, too, was planning a pilgrimage.

This evening when her work was finished she slipped out to

the garden and stood under the gnarled old olive tree to live over again the wonderful hour that had made life, her miserable, abused, unloved life, blossom into a holy devotion which crowded out all else. Only a bare week ago it had happened. She had been sent on a most surprising commission. Every few months Jonas used to climb upon the small donkey that lived in the shed off the inn room, and ride to Jerusalem with a basket of provisions for Sarah's old sister, old Anah, who was very poor. It seemed to Martha as if these trips used to come often, but of late they had become fewer and fewer. Jonas had stiff knees and stooped over now as he walked, and even the two-hour journey was too much for him.

So, three days before Passover, after much advice about the road and her errand and dire threats as to what would befall her when she returned if she did not fulfill all the instructions, she was started off on the donkey with the baskets of food and wine hanging from the saddle, on her first trip to Jerusalem!

The wonder and importance of it! She had wished as she rode along that the way might never end, for it meant freedom, and forgetfulness of the ills that made up her days. And then Jerusalem! Somewhere back in the hazy and beautiful past before she had mysteriously become a part of the inn, there had been a mother, she remembered, who had taught her sweet songs about it and talked of its great walls and gates and of the beauty of the holy Temple there. Now she was to see it for herself.

The narrow road was often rocky and steep, but the little donkey was sure-footed and travelled steadily. At the end of two hours she was in sight of the city on its high hills, with the soft blue-green of the Mount of Olives showing behind it, and farther to the east the Mountains of Moab, like towering fortresses of amethyst and sapphire in the late morning sun.

Her road led now up the sharp ravine on the western side, through the narrow passes, and at last through the great walls of which her mother had spoken, at the Joppa gate.

Once past the soldiers with their bright trappings and in the city, the strange scenes had become a blurred confusion of beggars and shouting merchants, of full-robed Pharisees and rabbis, and moving crowds of men and women and children.

After several frightened inquiries, she had found the Street of the Bakers, where Anah lived and had given her the food and wine. Then, after she had brought fresh water and ground some meal and told her all the news of the inn, she fed the donkey, ate the bread she had brought for herself and started off again through the narrow streets, her heart almost bursting with eagerness. She was going to see the Temple!

More timid inquiries here and there, and then at last—the great stone building with its long pillared colonnade and majestic gates came into view. She dismounted from the donkey and with a hand on its bridle made her way reverently toward the sacred spot.

Within a few rods of it a group of people blocked the way. They had been listening, evidently, to a rabbi and were waiting until He should speak again. Scarcely glancing at them, Martha tried with some impatience to skirt the crowd. Then a voice spoke, and, as though it had called her by name, she stopped wonderingly. Over the heads of the people she could hear it.

"A certain man planted a vineyard, and let it forth to husbandmen, and went into a far country."

It seemed to draw her as if a hand had reached out and caught her own. Cautiously she moved around the outer edge of the crowd, coming up at the side, quite near to the speaker. Then she saw His face. Tired, it looked, and sad, but oh, the infinite tenderness of it! Martha watched it with starving eyes.

He went on speaking to the people, while they quieted to listen. At last he had finished. The slender young man beside Him motioned the crowd away. Reluctantly they went. All but Martha. She was waiting for the voice to speak again, with her hungry eyes on the strange rabbi's face.

Suddenly He turned and saw her standing there, one arm about the small donkey's neck. His eyes read hers gravely, then He smiled and held out His hand.

"Thou art little Martha," He said.

And at the gentleness of it she found herself at His feet, sobbing out a wordless tale of the loneliness and weariness of her life with old Jonas and Sarah. Then she felt His hands on her head, and a peace and joy indescribable came over her.

"Fear not, little Martha; thou, too, shalt be my disciple.

She raised her eyes.

"Master," she breathed, "what is Thy name?"

"I am called Jesus," He said.

"*The Christ*," finished the fair young man, who still stood close beside Him.

Then she had kissed the blue and white tassels of His robe and come away, forgetting all about the Temple.

The same rocky road; the same harsh Jonas and Sarah at the end of it; the same inn with its hard duties from daylight till dark; but not the same Martha. He, the strange Master, had called her a disciple; His hands had been laid tenderly on her head in blessing.

One thought had gradually risen above all others. She longed to make Him a gift—something to show Him how much she loved Him. At first the idea brought only a sense of helplessness and despair. What had she, Martha of the inn, that she could give? She had lain awake a long time one night, watching the stars and wondering.

Then, as she sat beside the mill in the morning, grinding the wheat and barley, the idea came. She could make Him some little loaves. He had looked hungry and tired. She could take Him some bread. Oh, not the kind she made for use at the inn, but perfect loaves of the finest of the wheat. And she would go again to Jerusalem, as soon as the Passover week was over, and lay them in His hands.

Now, as she stood under the olive tree, her brows knitted in anxious thought, for there were many difficulties in the way and there were but two days left before the Sabbath. She had discovered that over the next hill there lived a man who had a wonderful kind of wheat which made flour as white as snow. But she had learned, too, that only the very rich went there to buy. She brooded hopelessly.

Then suddenly she remembered her one possession from the fair past to which the mother belonged—a gold chain, which for some reason Sarah had not taken from her. She loved to feel it and watch the shine of the gold, but it could go for the wheat if the man would accept it.

She would do the grinding after sundown on the Sabbath

when Jonas and Sarah had gone to the spring to gossip. Then very, very early on the first day of the week she would rise and bake the loaves and slip away on foot before they could miss her. She would not use the donkey, she decided. That belonged to Jonas, and this was not his errand. She could easily walk. It would all mean a frightful beating when she got back, but what did it matter if she had made her gift to the Master?

The next days, strangely enough for Martha, went as she had hoped they would. She had gone, undiscovered, with the gold chain to the man who had the fine wheat. He had looked surprised, then fingered the gold links covetously, and given her what

seemed a large sackful. She had returned, undiscovered, and hidden it in the garden in a broken part of the wall beneath the oleander tree.

The Sabbath came and dragged its burdensome length till sundown. Martha was trembling with eagerness and daring. Now was the time to begin the preparations. Jonas and Sarah left for the spring, where the old folks gathered in the evenings. Martha watched them out of sight, then worked feverishly. She took the sack from its hiding-place and seated herself with it at the mill, a shallow pot beside her to receive the flour.

She poured a few of the precious grains down the hole in the middle of the upper millstone, then ground slowly until the mill was thoroughly cleaned of the common flour still in it. Then, dusting the edges carefully, she poured more wheat and ground again, and then again and again, slowly, using all her strength upon the handle. The flour was as white as snow. She tested it softly between her thumb and finger. It was finer than any she had ever felt. It was almost worthy!

When it had all been placed in the pot she hid it carefully under a bushel measure in one corner of the inn room. She inspected the leaven, saved from the last week's baking. It still looked fresh and light. Then she went out for wood. She chose each piece with the greatest concern. Sometimes the smoke marred the loaves if the wood was too green. At last everything was done, even to selecting a fresh napkin in which to wrap the loaves and deciding upon the basket in which to carry them.

She went out to the garden and stood with her hands clasped on her breast, watching the Mountains of Moab, clothed in the purple and rose of the evening. Below them lay Jerusalem like a secret thing, hushed and hidden. Not a breath stirred the bright green leaves of the oleanders along the garden wall. Not a sound rose from the village. It seemed as if the whole world was still, waiting, dumbly expectant, breathlessly impatient, as she was, for the morrow.

When Jonas and Sarah returned Martha was already unrolling her pallet. Jonas drew the fastening of the door and they went on up to the roof-chamber where they slept.

A still, starry darkness crept on. Martha lay watching it through the small, open window. A strange stillness it was, soundless and yet athrob with mysterious anticipation as though angels might be hurrying past, unheard, unseen, but pressing softly, eagerly on toward Jerusalem.

Martha awoke, as she had prayed she might, very early—while it was yet dark. It was the first day of the week. It was her great day. In the twinkling of an eye she had slipped into her clothes, rolled up and put away her pallet and started her work. Into the clean baking-trough she poured the snowy flour, and mixed with it the salt and water and leaven, leaving it to rise while she built the fire in the oven. She moved softly, taking up and setting down each article with stealthy care. If Jonas or Sarah should wake? The fear was suffocating.

At the end of two hours the mists that had hung over the Mountains of Moab had broken into tiny feathers of cloud against the golden glory that had risen behind them.

The mountains gleamed with blue and amber. Over Jerusalem the light of the sunrise seemed to gather and spread as if, perchance, the hurrying angels of the night-time might now be risen to brood above the city with shining wings.

Martha bent over the small, low oven in an agony of hope and

fear, then lifted out the loaves with shaking hands. If there should be one mark, one blemish!

But there was not. In the full light of the doorway she realized with a trembling joy, past belief, that they were perfect. All four of them. White as snow, and light and even.

A stirring came from overhead. She caught up the fresh napkin and spread it in the basket. Upon it she laid the little loaves with exquisite care, folded it over them, and then fled out of the inn door and along the street in the direction of the shining light.

When Emmaus was left behind and she had started up the first long hill she stopped running and drew a long, shuddering breath of relief. She was safely on her way to the Master. Jonas and Sarah could not stop her now. And here in the basket were her gifts of love.

As she walked on she became aware of a new aliveness in the air about her. Every bird seemed to be singing. The very sky bent down like a warm, sentient thing. And over the steep hillsides, bright masses of anemones, scarlet and white and blue, breathed out the clear, living freshness of the morning as if they had all just been born into bloom. Martha's heart leaped at the beauty of it. Joy gave her strength and lightness of foot. Before she thought it possible she was entering once more the Joppa gate.

Her plan had been quite simple. She would find the Master, doubtless, near the Temple where He had been before. She would wait with the crowd and listen as long as He taught. Then when the others were all gone she would go up to Him and give Him the loaves.

When she came at last in sight of the Temple there were several groups of people in the street. She approached each and scanned it carefully before going on to the next. After a second patient searching the fearful certainty came that he was not there.

She was near the entrance of the Temple now, pausing uncertainly. One of the chief priests was walking back and forth along the corridors. She went close behind him.

"Hast thou seen Jesus, the Christ?" she asked timidly.

The great man started violently. His face was ashy grey. One arm shot threateningly toward her.

"Why askest thou *me?*" he shouted. *"Speak not that name to me! Begone!"*

Martha trembled with dismay as she ran away from the Temple

and down to the next street. What could the gentle Master have done to anger the priest so?

She continued her search. Everywhere people hurrying about their duties; here and there groups excitedly talking; but no sign of the rabbi and the young man who had stood beside Him. It was noon and Martha was hungry and tired. She must ask again or she would never find Him.

Two soldiers passed. She feared them, yet respected their power. Perhaps they could help her. She cautiously touched the arm of the one nearest her.

"Dost thou know where the rabbi Jesus is? They call Him the Christ."

The soldier looked at the other and laughed a strange, mirthless laugh. It pierced Martha's heart with a sense of impending doom.

"Hearest thou that?" he said loudly. "She asks us if we know aught of Jesus—we who helped crucify Him the other day."

From Martha's bloodless face her great dark eyes met the soldier's, agonized. He paused and spoke a little more softly:

"Thou hast the truth, child. He was crucified three days ago on Golgotha Hill. Devils they were who ordered it, but so it fell. Thou hast the truth."

They passed on. Martha leaned, sick and fainting, against the wall. *Crucified! Dead!* And in her basket were the little white loaves for Him. And He would never know. His hands would never touch them. The gentle Master, with only love and pity in His face—crucified! And the loaves were white as snow . . . perfect . . . to show her love for Him.

At last she roused herself and dragged her way wearily toward the Joppa gate.

A woman was sitting sadly in a doorway. She had a sweet,

patient face, and Martha halted, her heart lifting ever so little. One more inquiry; the soldier might have been mistaken.

"Didst thou know—Jesus?" she asked softly.

For answer the woman's reddened eyes overflowed. She rocked herself to and fro.

"And I trusted," she moaned, "that He was the redeemer of Israel. Some say today that He is alive again, risen; but it is only an idle tale. For I saw Him"—her voice sank to a choking whisper—"I saw Him die."

Martha moved slowly on, the woman rocking and moaning in the doorway.

The afternoon sun was hot now, and Martha's feet were heavy. The deep dust of the road rose to choke and blind her. The sharp stones tripped her and cut her feet. The way back was endless, for now there was no hope. She thought wearily of the freshness and joy of the morning. There would never be such beauty and happiness for her again. She stumbled on—and on.

When she reached the inn, at last, it was late afternoon. She was about to enter the main door when she caught her breath. No, she *could not* surrender the basket to Jonas and Sarah. Better to crush the little loaves in her hands and allow the birds of the air to have them.

She set the basket down beside the eastern door—Sarah rarely went out that way—then went to the front of the inn. With a shout they were both upon her.

"Thou shalt be taught to run away!" old Sarah cried. "Thou shalt be taught to go to Jerusalem without leave! Thou wast seen! It was told us!"

The blows came, as she had known they would. She had no strength to resist. She lay where she had fallen, beside the oven—the oven where only at daybreak she had laboured in ecstasy.

At last Jonas snarled: "It is there thou shouldst lie. It is there thou dost belong, under people's feet. But, hearken to this! If any shall come, thou shalt rise up and serve them. The caravans have long since passed, but if there should come a belated traveller rise up and serve him! Or thou shalt receive . . ."

He was still shaking his great fist as they went out.

Martha lay still. Soon, darkness; but not as of last night, filled with angels. Dead, despairing, empty darkness, tonight. She closed her eyes.

All at once there were footsteps along the street. Voices were talking earnestly. She recognized one of them. It was that of Cleopas, the rich vineyard owner. He always stopped at the inn on his trips to and from Jerusalem. A hand opened the door.

"Abide with us," she heard Cleopas say eagerly, "for the day is far spent."

Then they entered: Cleopas and his brother Simon, and another—a stranger, whose face was in the shadow.

Martha had risen with infinite pain and now set about placing the food upon the table. She brought the barley cakes and oil, the wine and the raisins, and the meal was ready. Then she stopped. Just outside the eastern door was the basket with its precious offering—the gift of love that could not be bestowed. Here were three men, weary from their journey and hungry.

The struggle in her breast was bitter but it was brief. She opened the door and lifted the basket. From their napkin she took the four loaves and placed them before the stranger, who sat in the shadows at the head of the table. Her eyes, dim with tears, watched the loaves as they lay there, snowy and fair. The longing love of her heart; the gold chain, her one treasure; her aching limbs; the swelling bruises on her poor beaten body; all these had helped to purchase them. She raised her eyes to the stranger's face–Then, a cry!

It was as though all the colour of the sunset and the radiance of the morning had united behind it. And out from the shining, majestic and glorified, yet yearning in its compassion and love, *The Face*, but not that of a stranger, appeared.

He was gazing steadfastly upon the little loaves. He touched them, broke them, extended them, and raised His eyes to heaven, while the blinding glory increased.

Cleopas and Simon were leaning forward, breathless, transfixed. Martha had crept closer and knelt within the circle of light.

"Master," she tried to whisper. "Master . . ."

He turned and looked upon her. No need to speak that which was upon her heart. He knew. He understood.

Gently the radiance enfolded her. Upon her shone the beneficent smile, fraught with heavenly benediction and healing for all earth's wounds.

Then, as softly as the sunset had gone, the celestial light died away. The Master's chair was empty.

Cleopas and Simon sat spellbound, gazing at the place where the splendour had been. Martha still knelt in a rapture of joy and peace.

On the table lay the little white loaves, uneaten, but received and blessed.

An Easter Wish

ANONYMOUS

May the glad dawn
Of Easter morn
Bring joy to thee.

May the calm eve
Of Easter leave
A peace divine with thee.

May Easter night
On thine heart write,
O Christ, I live for thee!

A Time of Rebirth

The Gospel According to St. Mark
15:22–37, 43–47, 16:1–15

KING JAMES VERSION

And they bring him unto the place Golgotha, which is, being interpreted, The place of a skull. And they gave him to drink wine mingled with myrrh: but he received it not. And when they had crucified him, they parted his garments, casting lots upon them, what every man should take. And it was the third hour, and they crucified him.

And when the sixth hour was come, there was darkness over the whole land until the ninth hour. And at the ninth hour Jesus cried with a loud voice, saying, Eloi, Eloi, lama sabachthani? which is, being interpreted, My God, my God, why hast thou forsaken me? And some of them that stood by, when they heard it, said, Behold, he calls Elias. And one ran and filled a spunge full of vinegar, and put it on a reed, and gave him to drink, saying, Let alone; let us see whether Elias will come to take him down. And Jesus cried with a loud voice, and gave up the ghost.

Joseph of Arimathaea, an honourable counsellor, which also waited for the kingdom of God, came, and went in boldly unto Pilate, and craved the body of Jesus. And Pilate marvelled if he were already dead: and calling unto him the centurion, he asked him whether he had been any while dead. And when he knew it of the centurion, he gave the body to Joseph. And he bought fine linen, and took him down, and wrapped him in the linen, and laid him in a sepulchre which was hewn out of a rock, and rolled a stone unto the door of the sepulchre. And Mary Magdalene and Mary the mother of Joses beheld where he was laid.

And when the sabbath was past, Mary Magdalene, and Mary the mother of James, and Salome, had bought sweet spices, that they might come and anoint him. And very early in the morning the first day of the week, they came unto the sepulchre at the rising of the sun. And they said among themselves, Who shall roll us away the stone from the door of the sepulchre? And when they looked, they saw that the stone was rolled away: for it was very great. And entering into the sepulchre, they saw a young man sitting on the right side, clothed in a long white garment; and they were affrighted. And he saith unto them, Be not affrighted: Ye seek Jesus of Nazareth, which was crucified: he is risen; he is not here: behold the place where they laid him. But go your way, tell his disciples and Peter that he goeth before you into Galilee: there shall ye see him, as he said unto you. And they went out quickly, and fled from the sepulchre; for they trembled and were amazed: neither said they any thing to any man; for they were afraid.

Now when Jesus was risen early the first day of the week, he appeared first to Mary Magdalene, out of whom he had cast seven devils. And she went and told them that had been with him, as they mourned and wept. And they, when they had heard that he was alive, and had been seen of her, believed not. After that he appeared in another form unto two of them, as they walked, and went into the country. And they went and told it unto the residue: neither believed they them. Afterward he appeared unto the eleven as they sat at meat, and upbraided them with their unbelief and hardness of heart, because they believed not them which had seen him after he was risen. And he said unto them, Go ye into all the world, and preach the gospel to every creature.

Easter

JOYCE KILMER

The air is like a butterfly
With frail blue wings.
The happy earth looks at the sky
And sings.

The Apple Tree

MARGERY WILLIAMS BIANCO

On winter days the children would put their faces close to the window pane and say: "If only it were spring!"

The window looked out on a little garden where in summer flowers bloomed, but now it was covered with snow. The lilac bushes stood up bare and stiff, and even the wild clematis wore a gray beard like an old man and seemed bowed down with the cold. Only the lame robin, who had stayed behind when all his friends flew southward, would come and hop near the doorsill, ruffling up his feathers, to peck for crumbs, and the tracks of his feet were like tiny hands in the snow.

Then their mother would say: "Cheer up, children! The winter is nearly over. Very soon Easter will be here, and then we shall have the birds and the flowers back again!"

The little sister asked: "When will it be really spring? I want it to be spring now!"

"When Easter comes," said their mother, "then it will be really spring."

"Does Easter come only in the spring?" the brother asked.

"Only in the spring."

"And suppose Easter never came at all!"

"That cannot happen," their mother answered, smiling. "Easter always comes, every year."

So day by day, from the window, the little brother and sister looked out up the road to see if Easter was coming. Nearly all the people who went by they knew by sight, neighbors who would turn their heads and wave a hand to the children as they neared the gate; very few strangers passed by on the road, and none of these looked like Easter.

"Perhaps he will come tomorrow," the brother always said.

"I think he will be dressed all in white," the little sister said, "and wear a shiny thing on his head, like the lady at the circus."

"No," said her brother. "He won't be like that at all. He will ride a big black horse, and he will have a helmet and a golden belt, and carry a sword in his hand."

"I don't want him to have a sword," the little sister said. "I'm afraid of swords!"

"That's only because you're a girl. Swords can't hurt you if you aren't afraid of them." And he began to talk about the kind of horse that Easter would ride, very proud and coal-black; it would lift its feet high at every step and have silver bells on the bridle.

The days passed, and presently the snow melted. The sun shone out, and little gray and pink buds showed on the tree branches. Now the lame robin was no longer as tame as he used to be; he came less often for crumbs, and instead was always flitting about the bushes, looking for the best spot to build a nest in when his family came back.

The children could play out of doors now, but they always kept an eye on the road, in case Easter should pass by when they weren't looking, for it would be dreadful to have waited all these weeks and then miss seeing him. Who knew but he might ride by in the night, and not stop at the cottage at all, especially if he were late and in a hurry?

And then one morning their mother stopped in her work to look at the calendar hanging on the wall by the fireplace, and exclaimed: "Why, how quickly the days do go by! Easter will be here before we know it!"

The children looked at each other and smiled.

"You see," the brother said. "He might come any minute now! We must be very careful!"

And so they always played in the front of the house, near the garden gate, where they could watch everyone who went past.

One day it really felt like spring. The sun seemed to shine more brightly than ever before; the sky was blue and the air soft and warm. Even the grass looked greener than usual, and all the new leaves on the lilac bushes had unfolded during the night. In the long grass by the gate there were dandelions in blossom.

"Easter will surely come today!" said the brother. "Let's go a little

way up the road, as far as the corner near the dead apple tree, and watch for him there."

So he took the little sister by the hand, and they went out through the gate and on to the road.

"I have saved a piece of bread in my pocket from breakfast," he told her. "So if you get hungry waiting we can sit down on the big stone by the tree and eat."

They set off, the little sister treading very carefully, for she was quite small, and where the path was stony she had to look first and see just where to put down each foot. Here and there along the edge of the road were tiny flowers, blue and white, and these the little sister wanted to stop and gather to give to Easter if they saw him. It took a long time; she gathered them quite short, with hardly any stalk, so that at every few steps they dropped from her hand and had to be picked up again. But the brother was very patient; he waited each time till she was ready to go on again, and in this way they came at last to the corner where the lane joined the high road.

It was market day in the town, and a number of people were going by on the highway, but they all looked hurried or tired or busy; there was no face among them all that seemed like the face that Easter would have, except one girl, bare-headed, who was singing as she walked. She alone turned her head to smile at the children, but before they could speak to her she had gone on her way.

Nowhere, up or down the road, could they see anyone who looked at all like Easter. One man rode by on a horse, but he had no sword, and he looked very cross, so the children were afraid to step out and ask him. But presently a workman came along with a bundle tied to a stick over his shoulder, and he stopped near the bank where the children were sitting to strike a light for his pipe.

"Could you tell me, please," the brother asked him, "whether Easter has gone by yet?"

"Why, no," said the workman slowly, staring at them. "Easter hasn't gone by yet, that I'm sure! I'm just going over to spend Easter day with my sister now. Over in the town where I've been working the folks don't set much store by Easter, but it's a holiday, so, thinks I, I'll pack up a few cakes for the little ones, and here I am. They'll be looking out for me surely! I wrote a letter to my sister a week ago, telling her. Just so sure as Easter comes, I said, I'll be there!"

"Then you know what Easter's like?" asked the brother.

"That I do!" said the workman. "Back in the country, when I was a boy, all the folks round about kept Easter, and we made a great feast every year. And that's why I'm going over to my sister's now, for the sake of old times, and to fetch the children a few cakes for the holiday. I'd give you some, and gladly, but it's a big family there and times are hard, so I was able to get only one apiece, all round, but that's better than nothing. Still, I slipped an apple or two in my pocket, coming along, and maybe you'd like them instead."

He pulled two big red apples out of his pocket and gave one to each of them.

"That's better than nothing," he said again as the children thanked him. "And now I must be getting on."

"Perhaps," said the brother, "you'll meet Easter on the road, if he hasn't gone by yet. Do you think you will?"

The workman laughed as if that were a great joke.

"Why, if I don't hurry up," he said, "I surely will! For it's all of twelve miles yet to my sister's house, and I just reckoned to get there by nightfall. So good-by, and a happy Easter to you both!"

He went off up the road, whistling, and walking very fast.

"Oh, dear," sighed the little sister, "I wish Easter would come quickly! I'm so tired of waiting!"

"We'll wait a little longer," said her brother, "and then we will go back and eat our lunch by the stone under the apple tree." For he too was beginning to feel rather tired of waiting there by the road-side. "You see, if there are so many people who want to keep Easter, that must make it hard for him to get about, and then it isn't his fault that he's late. Perhaps there is someone keeping him now, this very minute, and that's why he hasn't come. Of course, if he has a horse that would make it easier."

He thought of Easter, on a big black horse, riding through the villages, perhaps this very minute, and all the people stretching out their hands to stop him, and wanting him to stay with them. And the black horse tossing his head, to set all the silver bells ringing. It would be a fine thing to travel round with Easter, to walk by his side on the road and hold his horse whenever he dismounted. But the little sister thought of home, and a bowl of bread and milk, for she was getting sleepy.

The road was empty now; for a long while no one had passed up or down. But at last, very far in the distance, they could see someone moving. Under the hot, still rays of the sun, drawing the spring moisture from the earth, the air seemed to tremble; distant objects, a line of poplar trees, the red-roofed farmhouse by the hill, even the surface of the road, blended and swam together, so that the brother, shading his eyes to gaze up the highway, could not be sure if what he saw was really a figure on a horse and the flash of gold and silver trappings, or just a cloud of dust gilded by the sunlight.

For a moment he thought he heard music, distant trumpets and the shouting of many voices, and then he knew that what he really heard was only the jingle of a sheep bell in the pasture and the crying of rooks on the plowed field, and that what he saw was no horse and rider, but only someone on foot coming toward him along the road. And when the figure drew quite near he saw that it was a man, dressed in shabby clothes and walking slowly, as though he had come a long way on foot and was very weary. But when he saw the children he stopped to smile at them, and his smile was friendly.

"Are you waiting for someone?" he asked. "For I saw you from a long way off, looking out up the road."

"We were waiting for someone," said the brother, "but I'm afraid he can't be coming today, we have waited so long, and I think we will go back now and eat our bread under the tree, for my sister is getting tired."

"I'm tired, too," the stranger said, "so if I may, I will come with you. Look, your little sister is nearly asleep!"

He picked the little sister up in his arms as he spoke. She was hot and tired and disappointed, and just getting ready to cry, but she put her head down on the man's shoulder and clung round his neck, for he held her like a person who is used to carrying little children. So they went, all three of them, back to the turn of the road and down the lane to where the apple tree grew.

• • •

It was quite an old tree, and for many years now it had not borne any blossom. Only a few twisted leaves came on it every spring, and these soon withered and dropped. It was good to cut down for firewood, the farmer said, but the months passed and no one found the time to cut it, so it had been left standing there. The bare gnarled branches made a good-enough shade in the spring, and just beneath it was a big flat stone, comfortable to sit on, and near the stone a little trickling spring of water.

They sat down, the man with his back against the tree and the boy near him, and the little sister, who had forgotten her tiredness now, sat with her thumb in her mouth and looked at them both.

"I'm sorry I've only got a little piece of bread," said the brother, rather shyly, for he thought that perhaps the man was really a beggar, he was so poorly dressed, and in that case he might be quite hungry. "If I'd known, I would have brought more."

"I expect it will be enough for all of us," the man said. And when he took the slice of bread from the brother's hand it certainly did seem larger than one had thought; he broke it into three pieces, and there was quite enough for all of them, as much as they wanted to eat. And it tasted wonderfully good, the brother thought; by far the best bread his mother had ever baked, but perhaps that was because he was so hungry.

They drank from the spring, and the man showed them how to make cups out of leaves, fastened with a thorn, that would hold the water. And after that he told them stories, jolly stories about the little reed that grew down in the ditch and wanted to be an oak tree, and about the king's son who had a dream, and who threw his crown away and went out into the world and became a beggar. He seemed to be a very nice man indeed, and the children were glad they had met him.

"You must have come a very long way," said the brother presently. For he couldn't help noticing how dusty the man's feet were and that his clothes were quite worn.

"I have come a long way," the man said, "and I have still a long way to go."

"Is your home very far?"

"I have no home," he said. "Sometimes I find friends with whom I can stay for a little while, and they give me shelter. And there are others, good-hearted people, who think they want me, and ask me into their houses, but they don't really want me; they have business to look after and many things to do, and after a while they find I'm only a trouble to them, and out of place in their households, and they can't spare the time for me, and so I have to go."

"Do you never go back?" asked the brother.

"Yes, if someone dies or there is real trouble in the house and no one else to turn to, then they may remember and send for me, or they just leave the door ajar so I can come in."

"It must be a fine thing to travel all over the world," said the brother. He thought again of Easter and the tall black horse. "Wouldn't it be splendid to be a king? And then you would ride into the city and all the bells would ring and the people come out to meet you."

But the man didn't answer. Perhaps he hadn't heard, or was thinking of something else.

"Did you ever ride on a horse and have a sword?" the brother asked.

"I had a sword once," said the man, "but I gave it away."

"Weren't you sorry afterward?"

But again the man didn't answer; he was murmuring something, looking down on the earth at his feet, and the brother thought: Perhaps he really is sorry about the sword and doesn't like to speak of it. It was something one shouldn't have asked, and he didn't want to hurt the man's feelings. So he said aloud:

"Won't you tell us about some of the fine things you saw when you were traveling?"

The man looked up and smiled at them, and he put his hand inside the torn lining of his coat.

"This," he said, "is the most precious thing that I have found to-day, and I picked it up by the roadside."

He drew out his hand carefully; something very wonderful must be there, the boy thought, a tiny carved casket, or perhaps a jewel someone had dropped. But when he spread his fingers there was only a little brown bird on his hand, quite dead and limp, with its feathers ruffled, all dusty from lying in the road. The boy was disappointed; it wasn't at all what he expected to see, but the little sister reached out her hand.

"It's a bird!" she cried. "It's a dear little bird, and I don't want it to be dead!"

She stroked it with her tiny fingers as it lay on the man's hand, and there were tears in her eyes.

"Don't cry," said the man. "See, we both love the little bird, and I am going to show you something!"

He held the little dead sparrow close to his face, while the child watched, and breathed on it; something seemed to stir between his fingers, and when he opened his hand the bird flew away. Straight

up in the air it flew, spreading its wings, and as the little sister looked up at it it seemed to change. She thought it had been brown, but now it was snow-white all over, like a white dove, and it hovered a moment above them, and then was gone, far up in the blue sky, but she thought she heard it singing as it flew.

The brother stared. "Where did it go?" he cried. "I saw it lying on your hand and then it wasn't there!"

"It flew away," said the little sister.

"It was dead," said her brother, "and dead things cannot fly."

"I tell you it flew," the little sister repeated. "It flew into the sky, and I saw it!"

And she came near and put her arms round the man's neck and kissed him. "You are a nice man," she said, "and you shall have all the flowers that I gather for Easter, for you are much nicer than Easter, and no one must ever be unkind to you, because I love you. And I want you to live with us always."

And she looked at him again, and this time she said: "I think you are Easter, for I see a shiny thing on your head."

But though the brother looked, he saw only the sun shining through the branches of the apple tree.

"You are a kind man," he said, "even if you aren't Easter, and some day I hope you will come again and tell us some more stories, for I like your stories very much. And when I grow up and have a sword of my own I am going to give it to you."

They went home, and left the man sitting there under the apple tree. His head leaned back against the tree trunk and his arms were outstretched and he seemed to be sleeping, and in his open hand lay the flowers the little sister had given him. But perhaps he was only resting, for he must have been very tired still.

"I tell you he is Easter," the little sister said. "He is just like I said he would be."

"He isn't Easter," said her brother, "but he is a very nice man, and I am sorry he has to walk so far."

But the little sister pulled at his hand, standing still in the road. "Don't you see?" she cried. "There is something shining round his head, like gold, and look—the apple tree is all in flower!"

The brother looked.

"It is only the setting sun," he said. "There is no blossom on the tree, for I looked this morning. But tomorrow we'll come back and see."

In the morning, when the children went back to look, the man had gone. But it was as the little sister had said; the apple tree that had been withered for so many years was in flower. The boughs, covered with pink-and-white blossom, stretched out against the blue sky in blessing and their perfume filled the air all about.

It was really spring; the birds were singing and far away, as the children stood under the apple tree, they could hear the bells ringing for Easter.

The Waking Year

EMILY DICKINSON

A lady red upon the hill
    Her annual secret keeps;
A lady white within the field
    In placid lily sleeps!

The tidy breezes with their brooms
    Sweep vale, and hill, and tree!
Prithee, my pretty housewives!
    Who may expected be?

The neighbors do not yet suspect!
    The woods exchange a smile–
Orchard, and buttercup, and bird–
    In such a little while!

And yet how still the landscape stands,
    How nonchalant the wood,
As if the resurrection
    Were nothing very odd!

Spring

WILLIAM BLAKE

Sound the flute!
Now it's mute.
Birds delight
Day and night;
Nightingale
In the dale,
Lark in sky,
Merrily,
Merrily, merrily, to welcome in the year.
Little boy,
Full of joy;
Little girl,
Sweet and small;
Cock does crow,
So do you;
Merry voice,
Infant noise,
Merrily, merrily, to welcome in the year.
Little lamb,
Here I am;
Come and lick
My white neck;
Let me pull
Your soft wool;
Let me kiss
Your soft face:
Merrily, merrily, to welcome in the year.

The Boy Who Discovered the Spring

RAYMOND MacDONALD ALDEN

There came once a little Elf Boy to live on this earth, and he was so much pleased with it that he stayed, never caring to go back to his own world. I do not know where his own world was, or just how he came to leave it. Some thought that he was dropped by accident from some falling star, and some that he had flown away, thinking that he could fly back again whenever he chose, because he did not know that children always lose their wings when they come into this world. But no one knew certainly, as he never told any one; and, after all, it did not matter, since, as I have already said, he liked the earth so much that he did not care to leave it.

There was a Hermit who lived in the valley where the little Boy had first come, and, as he had a room in his house for a visitor, he took him in, and they grew to like each other so well that again the little Boy did not care to go away, nor did the Hermit care to have him. The Hermit had not always been a Hermit, but he had become a sorrowful man, and did not care to live where other people lived, or to share any of their pleasures. The reason he had become a sorrowful man was that his only child had died, and it seemed to him that there was nothing worth living for after that. So he moved to the lonely valley, and I suppose would have spent the rest of his life by himself, if it had not been for the little Elf Boy.

It was a very lovely valley, with great, green meadows that sloped down to a rippling brook, and in summertime were full of red and white and yellow blossoms. Over the brook there hung green trees, whose roots made pleasant places to rest when one was tired; and along the water's edge there grew blue flowers, while many little frogs and other live creatures played there. It was summertime when the little Elf Boy came, and the flowers and the trees and the brook and the frogs made him very happy. I think that in the world from which he came they did not have such things: It was made chiefly of gold and silver and precious stones, instead of things that grow and blossom and keep one company. So the Elf Boy was very happy. He did not ask to go to play in the village over the hill, but was quite content with the meadows and

the brook-side. The only thing that did not please him was that the old Hermit still remained sorrowful, thinking always of his child who had died; and this the Elf Boy did not understand, for in the world from which he came nothing ever died, and he thought it strange that if the Hermit's child had died he did not patiently wait for him to come back again.

So the summer went merrily on, and the Elf Boy learned to know the names of all the flowers in the meadow, and to love them dearly. He also became so well acquainted with the birds that they would come to him for crumbs, and sit on the branches close by to sing to him; the frogs would do the same thing, and although the Elf Boy did not think their voices as sweet as those of the birds, he was too polite to let them know it.

But when September came, there began to be a sad change. The first thing the Elf Boy noticed was that the birds began to disappear from the meadows. When he complained of this, the Hermit told him they had gone to make their visit to the Southland, and would come back again; and this he easily believed. But as time went on, and the air became more and more still as the last of them took their flight, he began to lose heart.

What was worse, at the same time the flowers began to disappear from the meadows. They were dead, the Hermit said, and in this way the Elf Boy learned what that meant. At first others came to take their places, and he tried to learn to like the flowers of autumn as well as those which he had known first. But as these faded and dropped off, none came after them. The mornings grew colder, and the leaves on the trees were changing in a strange way. When they grew red and yellow, instead of green, the Elf Boy thought it was a queer thing for them to put on different colors, and wondered how long it would last. But when they began to fall, he was very sad indeed. At last there came a day when every limb was bare, except for a few dried leaves at the top of one of the tallest trees. The Elf Boy was almost broken-hearted.

One morning he went out early, to see what new and dreadful thing had happened in the night, for it seemed now that every night took something beautiful out of the world. He made his way toward the brook, but when he reached the place where he usually heard it calling to him as it ran merrily over the stones, he could not hear a sound. He stopped and listened, but everything was wonderfully still. Then he ran as fast as his feet would carry him to the border of the brook. Sure enough, it had stopped running. It was covered with a hard sheet of ice.

The Elf Boy turned and went to the Hermit's house. By the time he had reached it, the tears were running down his cheeks.

"Why, what is the matter?" asked the Hermit.

"The brook is dead," said the Elf Boy.

"I think not," said the Hermit. "It is frozen over, but that will not hurt it. Be patient, and it will sing to you again."

"No," said the Elf Boy. "You told me that the birds would come back, and they have not come. You told me that the trees were not dead, but their leaves have every one gone, and I am sure they are. You told me that the flowers had seeds that did not die, but would make other flowers; but I can not find them, and the meadow is bare and dark. Even the grass is not green any more. It is a dead world. In the summertime I did not see how you could be sorrowful; but now I do not see how any one can be happy."

The Hermit thought it would be of no use to try to explain anything more to the Elf Boy; so he said again, "Be patient," and tried to find some books in which he could teach the Boy to read, and make him forget the outside world.

The next time they went for a walk to the village over the hill, the Elf Boy was very curious to see whether the same thing had happened there that had happened in their valley. Of course it had: The trees there seemed dead, too, and the flowers were all gone from the door-yards. The Boy expected that every one in the village would now be as sorrowful as the Hermit, and he was very much surprised when he saw them looking as cheerful as ever. There were some boys playing on the street corner, who seemed to be as happy as boys could be. One of them spoke to the Elf Boy, and he answered, "How can you play so happily, when such a dreadful thing has happened to the world?"

"Why, what has happened?"

"The flowers and trees are dead," said the Elf Boy, "and the birds are gone, and the brook is frozen, and the meadow is bare and gray. And it is so on this side of the hill also."

Then the boys in the street laughed merrily, and did not answer the Elf Boy, for they remembered that he was a stranger in the world, and supposed he would not understand if they should try to talk to him. And he went on through the village, not daring to speak to any others, but all the time wondering that the people could still be so happy.

As the winter came on, the Hermit taught him many things from the books in his house, and the Elf Boy grew interested in them and was not always sad. When the snow came he found ways to play in it, and even saw that the meadow was beautiful again, though in a different way from what it had been in summer. Yet still he could not think the world by any means so pleasant a place as it had been in the time of flowers and birds; and if it were not that he had become very fond of the Hermit, who was now the

only friend he could remember, he would have wished to go back to the world from which he had come. It seemed to him now that the Hermit must miss him very much if he should go away, since they two were the only people who seemed really to understand how sorrowful a place the earth is.

So the weeks went by. One day in March, as he and the Hermit sat at their books, drops of water began to fall from the eaves of the roof, and they saw that the snow was melting in the sunshine.

"Do you want to take a little walk down toward the brook?" asked the Hermit. "I should not wonder if I could prove to you to-day that it has not forgotten how to talk to you."

"Yes," said the Elf Boy, though he did not think the Hermit could be right. It was months since he had cared to visit the brook, it made him so sad to find it still and cold.

When they reached the foot of the hillside the sheet of ice was still there, as he had expected.

"Never mind," said the Hermit. "Come out on the ice with me, and put down your ear and listen."

So the Elf Boy put down his ear and listened; and he heard, as plainly as though there were no ice between, the voice of the brook gurgling in the bottom of its bed. He clapped his hands for joy.

"It is waking up, you see," said the Hermit. "Other things will waken too, if you will be patient."

The Elf Boy did not know quite what to think, but he waited day after day with his eyes and ears wide open to see if anything else might happen; and wonderful things did happen all the time. The brook sang more and more distinctly, and at last broke through its cold coverlet and went dancing along in full sight. One morning, while the snow was still around the house, the Elf Boy heard a chirping sound, and, looking from his window, saw a red robin outside asking for his breakfast.

"Why," cried the Boy, "have you really come back again?"

"Certainly," said the robin, "don't you know it is almost spring?"

But the Elf Boy did not understand what he said.

There was a pussy-willow growing by the brook, and the Boy's next discovery was that hundreds of little gray buds were coming out. He watched them grow bigger from day to day, and while he was doing this the snow was melting away in great patches where the sun shone warmest on the meadow, and the blades of grass that came up into the daylight were greener than anything the Elf Boy had ever seen.

Then the pink buds came on the maple trees, and unfolded day by day. And the fruit trees in the Hermit's orchard were as white with blossoms as they had lately been with snow.

"Not a single tree is dead," said the Elf Boy.

Last of all came the wild flowers—blue and white violets near the brook, dandelions around the house, and, a little later, yellow buttercups all over the meadow. Slowly but steadily the world was made over, until it glowed with white and green and gold.

The Elf Boy was wild with joy. One by one his old friends came back, and he could not bear to stay in the house for many minutes from morning to night. Now he knew what the wise Hermit had meant by saying, "Be patient;" and he began to wonder again that the Hermit could be sorrowful in so beautiful a world.

One morning the church bells in the village—whose ringing was the only sound that ever came from the village over the hill— rang so much longer and more joyfully than usual, that the Elf Boy asked the Hermit why they did so. The Hermit looked in one of his books, and answered:

"It is Easter Day. The village people celebrate it on one Sunday every spring."

"May we not go also?" asked the Elf Boy, and as it was the first time he had ever asked to go to the village, the Hermit could not refuse to take him.

The village was glowing with flowers. There were many fruit trees, and they, too, were in blossom. Every one who passed along the street seemed either to wear flowers or to carry them in his hand. The people were all entering the churchyard; and here the graves, which had looked so gray and cold when the Hermit and the Boy had last seen them, were beautiful with flowers that the village people had planted or had strewn over them for Easter.

The people all passed into the church. But the Hermit and the Elf Boy, who never went where there was a crowd, stayed outside where the hummingbirds and bees were flying happily among the flowers. Suddenly there came from the church a burst of music. To the Elf Boy it seemed the most beautiful sound he had ever heard. He put his finger on his lip to show the Hermit that he wanted to listen. These were the words they sang:

"I am He that liveth, and was dead; and, behold, I am alive for evermore!"

The Boy took hold of the Hermit's hand and led him to the church door, that they might hear still better. He was very happy.

"Oh," he cried, "I do not believe that anything ever really dies."

The Hermit looked down at him and smiled. "Perhaps not," he said.

When the music began again, a strange thing happened. The Hermit sang the Easter song with the others. It was the first time he had sung for many years.

Spring Song

LUCILLE CLIFTON

the green of Jesus
is breaking the ground
and the sweet
smell of delicious Jesus
is opening the house and
the dance of Jesus music
has hold of the air and
the world is turning
in the body of Jesus and
the future is possible

A Time of Celebration

The Gospel According to St. Matthew
27: 30–36, 46–50, 57–60, 28:1–10, 16–20

KING JAMES VERSION

And they spit upon him, and took the reed, and smote him on the head. And after that they had mocked him, they took the robe off from him, and put his own rainment on him, and led him away to crucify him. And as they came out, they found a man of Cyrene, Simon by name: him they compelled to bear his cross. And when they were come unto a place called Golgotha, that is to say, a place of a skull, They gave him vinegar to drink mingled with gall: and when he had tasted thereof, he would not drink. And they crucified him, and parted his garments, casting lots: that it might be fulfilled which was spoken by the prophet, They parted my garments among them, and upon my vesture did they cast lots. And sitting down they watched him there. And about the ninth hour Jesus cried with a loud voice, saying, Eli, Eli, lama sabachthani? that is to say, My God, my God, why hast thou forsaken me? Some of them that stood there, when they heard that, said, This man calleth for Elias. And straightway one of them ran, and took a spunge, and filled it with vinegar, and put it on a reed, and gave him to drink.

The rest said, Let be, let us see whether Elias will come to save him.

Jesus, when he had cried again with a loud voice, yielded up the ghost.

When the even was come, there came a rich man of Arimathaea, named Joseph, who also himself was Jesus' disciple: He went to Pilate, and begged the body of Jesus. Then Pilate

commanded the body to be delivered. And when Joseph had taken the body, he wrapped it in a clean linen cloth, and laid it in his own new tomb, which he had hewn out in the rock: and he rolled a great stone to the door of the sepulchre, and departed.

In the end of the sabbath, as it began to dawn toward the first day of the week, came Mary Magdalene and the other Mary to see the sepulchre. And, behold, there was a great earthquake: for the angel of the Lord descended from heaven, and came and rolled back the stone from the door, and sat upon it. His countenance was like lightning, and his raiment white as snow: And for fear of him the keepers did shake, and became as dead men. And the angel answered and said unto the women, Fear not ye: for I know that ye seek Jesus, which was crucified. He is not here: for he is risen, as he said. Come, see the place where the Lord lay. And go quickly, and tell his disciples that he is risen from the dead; and, behold, he goeth before you into Galilee; there shall ye see him: lo, I have told you. And they departed quickly from the sepulchre with fear and great joy; and did run to bring his disciples word. And as they went to tell his disciples, behold, Jesus met them, saying, All hail. And they came and held him by the feet, and worshipped him. Then said Jesus unto them, Be not afraid: go tell my brethren that they go into Galilee, and there shall they see me.

Then the eleven disciples went away into Galilee, into a mountain where Jesus had appointed them. And when they saw him, they worshipped him: but some doubted. And Jesus came and spake unto them, saying, All power is given unto me in heaven and in earth. Go ye therefore, and teach all nations, baptizing them in the name of the Father, and of the Son, and of the Holy Ghost: Teaching them to observe all things whatsoever I have commanded you: and, lo, I am with you alway, even unto the end of the world. Amen.

Easter's Coming

AILEEN FISHER

Through the sunshine,
through the shadow,
down the hillside,
down the meadow,
little streams
run bright and merry,
bursting with the news
they carry,
singing, shouting,
laughing, humming,
"Easter's coming,
Easter's coming!"

Hot-Cross Buns!

Hot-cross buns! Hot-cross buns!
One a penny, two a penny,
Hot-cross buns!
If you have no daughters,
Give them to your sons,
One a penny, two a penny,
Hot-cross buns!

In the Easter Basket

ELIZABETH HOUGH SECHRIST

Early on Easter morning thousands of small boys and girls scramble out of bed in a hurry to see what the Easter rabbit has brought them. And what do many of them find? A gay wicker basket, with colored straw forming a nest, and the nest piled so high that the basket is fairly bursting with Easter eggs and chocolate rabbits and little marshmallow chicks!

The Easter eggs vary, from the huge chocolate cream egg with the child's name written on it in white or pink icing, all decorated with fancy pink and green and white rosettes, to the colored hens' eggs and luscious fruit and nut eggs and marshmallow eggs of every hue, and the bittersweet chocolate ones that are hollow inside, down to the very tiny gelatin eggs known as jelly beans, of every color in the rainbow, dripping down through the straw!

Sometimes, too, there's an old-fashioned egg that may have belonged to Grandma. This is the most interesting egg of all. It's made of frosted glass, hollow inside and containing a little round window through which, if you squint one eye, you can see a miniature garden of flowers with perhaps some bluebirds flying above.

But why are there all these Easter eggs and chocolate bunnies at Easter, and why are the children told that the Easter bunny has brought them? There is a reason.

First of all, let us take the case of the Easter rabbit. The rabbit is also called a hare. According to Egyptian mythology the hare is a symbol of the moon. It is thought that its significance at Easter is its association with the date of the festival, for that date is determined by the moon. When the Christian fathers met at the Council of Nicaea back in the year 325, the date of Easter was definitely settled and has been kept by their ruling ever since.

It was decided that Easter should be kept upon the first Sunday after the first *full moon* following the twenty-first day of March. And so the hare, representing the moon, came to be associated with the Easter festival.

For hundreds of years, in certain sections of England, hare hunts have been held on Easter. An ancient custom in the County of Warwick had to do with the Easter hare. If this little animal could be caught and taken to the village parson before ten o'clock on Easter morning, the parson, in return, was obliged to give the young people who caught it a hundred eggs for breakfast!

In Germany, Switzerland, and Belgium the boys and girls put nests in the grass in their gardens so that the Easter rabbit may fill them with eggs. But if the weather turns out to be unpleasant, the rabbit finds places inside the house to hide the eggs. In Italy bunny-shaped pastries are baked for the Easter feast.

As for the Easter eggs! They are so closely related to the festival all over the Christian world that Easter would not seem right without them. Even before the time of Christ it was customary to exchange eggs. The Hebrews, for hundreds of years, have included the Paschal egg at the feast of the Passover. The ancient peoples of Egypt, Persia, Greece, and Rome followed the custom of exchanging eggs at their spring festivals. In Babylonia eggs were presented to the ancient goddess of fertility, Astarte.

A very old Hindu myth told how the world itself was created from a giant world-egg. After the mammoth egg had lain dormant for a period of time, the story went, it finally split into two halves, the earth and the sky. To people of all ages the egg has represented new life. And so Christian people have welcomed it at the celebration of Easter as a sign of the Resurrection, the new birth in the risen Lord.

In Ireland the fast of Lent is broken at dawn on Easter day by eating a meal of eggs.

It is the custom in some parts of France for the children to take gifts of eggs to the priest when they go to church on Holy Saturday to make confession. In that country, in days gone by, egg races were held at the Easter fetes. The prize for the winner was a hogshead of cider! All over Europe egg races are popular at Easter time. The eggs are saved carefully by the children throughout Holy Week.

English children are presented with gifts of chocolate eggs wrapped in fancy colored paper. In Austrian or German families presents are often given to the children concealed within an imitation Easter egg. The little egg-shaped boxes are saved and used all year to hold trinkets. In Germany it is thought to bring good luck to carry a green-colored egg on the person on Maundy Thursday.

Through the years many methods of coloring eggs were used by the country people to whom commercial dyes were not available. They made use of onion skins, herb juices, furze (a shrub with yellow flowers), various species of flowers, and bits of colored cloth soaked in hot water to bring out the dye color.

In the Tyrol the children collect eggs on Easter eve. They go about from farmhouse to farmhouse singing carols. They carry baskets with them, and into the baskets go the gifts of Easter eggs from the farmers' wives as reward for their songs. The eggs have been specially prepared for the children, all dyed in bright colors and decorated. Some of them have religious mottoes printed on them.

In England, long ago, messages were often written on the eggs that were sent to friends and relatives. It sometimes happened that years later these eggs, if the date had appeared on them, were used for proof in establishing facts in family records.

Italian families bake a special round cake for the holy day which they decorate with Easter eggs. The Italians take their eggs to church on Easter eve, where they are blessed by the priest. At the Easter feast next day these eggs are placed in the center of the table with everything else arranged around them.

What a lot of them there are! Sometimes as many as two hundred, all of them colored in the gayest colors! There are so many because everyone who enters the house during the holidays is offered at least one egg, and no one may refuse this token of the

Resurrection. The custom of paying calls on the afternoon of Easter Sunday is very popular in southern Europe. Children look forward to it because at each place they are given Easter eggs and sweets.

In the Czech Republic eggs are given to pay a forfeit. On Easter Monday the boys make fancy, decorated willow whips and pretend to switch the girls with them! This is supposed to bring good luck to the girls, so they reward the boys with gaily decorated eggs.

In Bosnia and Herzegovina and in other places where the Slavic people live, it is the custom to prepare great quantities of eggs on Great Thursday. Some of the eggs are dyed black and are placed on the graves of departed members of the family. In Greece and Romania the eggs are colored red to express the joy of the Easter season. When friends meet on Easter Day, each knocks a red egg against the egg of the other person, and the greeting "Christ is risen!" is exchanged, with the reply, "Truly. He is risen."

Red eggs are popular also in the Ukraine. Young girls rub their cheeks with them on Easter for a rosy appearance. Nowhere else in the world, probably, are there such beautiful Easter eggs as in the villages of the Ukraine. For generations the villagers have made up their own designs, using homemade tools and dyes for the intricate work. The designs feature chapels, belfries, priests' robes, fir trees, and other interesting subjects.

The eggs, along with other Easter foods, are blessed by the priest on the eve of Easter, then taken home for the feast on the morrow. The Ukrainians cast the shells of some of their eggs upon the waters in honor of the dead.

Bulgarian families, who prefer red Easter eggs, always place the first decorated egg before the family icon as a symbol of the Resurrection.

Empty eggshells are used in several European countries for

decoration and display on Easter Day. The uncooked egg is pierced with a needle at each end and the contents are blown out. Easter-egg trees made of these hollow eggshells are especially popular in Germany. The decorated shells are suspended from a branch or from a small tree. Then the Easter-egg tree is placed on a table in a prominent place, where it is admired by visitors to the house.

In Norway the children use empty eggshells to make tiny baskets for holding small candies. Sometimes these are pasted shut after they are filled and are then hidden in nests to be found on Easter morning.

Easter-egg trees have become popular in our own country, too. These and other Easter traditions have come to us from lands across the seas. One such custom came from Germany and Norway. It is the egg-rolling party that is given annually on Easter Monday on the lawn of the White House in the nation's capital. The wife of the President of the United States is the hostess. The party is attended by hundreds of eager children, each carrying a basket of colored eggs for the rolling. In all the running and tumbling and happy shouting that follow, no one stops to realize that this is a sport that has been popular for many, many years.

Egg rolling, Easter-egg trees, nests of eggs hidden in the garden, Easter baskets found early on Easter morning—all these have a truly important place in the Easter celebration. Boys and girls have been enjoying them for hundreds of years in the past. Let us hope they will stay with us for many years to come!

The Easter Parade

WILLIAM JAY SMITH

What shall I wear for the Easter Parade?
A dress that's the color of marmalade
With a border embroidered in light blue cornflowers
Like the edge of a meadow after spring showers
And a matching hat round as a top you can spin
And elastic to hold it on under my chin
And brand-new shoes whiter than newly-poured cream
With heart-shaped, golden buckles that gleam
And I'll carry a small purse of butterfly blue
With a penny for me and a penny for you
To buy us both glasses of cold lemonade
When we walk, hand in hand, in the Easter Parade.

Why the Easter Bunny Lays Eggs

F. E. CORNE

Part I

Many hundred years ago, a good and noble lady, Duchess Rosilinda von Lindenburg, at a time when a cruel war was devastating the land, was obliged to fly from her beautiful home accompanied only by her two little children and one old manservant.

They found refuge in a small mining village in the mountains, where the simple but contented and happy inhabitants did what they could for their comfort, and placed the best of all they had at the disposal of the wanderers. Nevertheless, their fare was miserable; no meat was ever to be found, seldom fish, and not even an egg; this last for the very good reason that there was not a single hen in the village! These useful domestic fowls, now so common everywhere, were originally brought from the East, and had not yet found their way to this secluded place. The people had not even heard of such "strange birds." This troubled the kind duchess, who well knew the great help they are in housekeeping, and she determined that the women who had been so kind to her should no longer be without them.

Accordingly, the next time she sent forth her faithful old servant to try and gather news of his master and of the progress of the war, she commissioned him to bring back with him a coop full of fowls. This he did, to the great surprise of the simple natives, and the village children were greatly excited a few weeks later at the

appearance of a brood of young chickens. They were so pretty and bright, were covered with such a soft down, were so open-eyed, and could run about after their mother to pick up food the very first day, and were altogether such a contrast to the blind, bald, un-fledged, helpless, ugly little birds they sometimes saw in nests in the hedges, that they could not find words enough to express their admiration.

Part II

The good lady now saved up eggs for some time, then invited all the housewives of the village to a feast, when she set before them eggs cooked in a variety of ways. She then taught them how to prepare them for themselves, and, distributing a number of fowls among them, sent the dames home grateful and happy.

When Easter approached, she was anxious to arrange some pleasure for the village children, but had nothing to give them, "not even an apple or a nut," only some eggs; but that, she concluded, was, after all, an appropriate offering, "as an egg is the first gift of the reviving spring." And then it occurred to her to boil them with mosses and roots that would give them a variety of brilliant colors, "as the earth," said she, "has just laid aside her white mantle, and decorated herself with many colors; for the dear God makes the fruit and berries not only good to eat, but also pleasant to look upon," and the children's pleasure would be all the greater.

Accordingly, on Easter Sunday, after the church service, all the little ones of about the age of her own met together in a garden; and, when their kind hostess had talked to them a while, she led them into a small neighboring wood. There she told them to make nests of moss, and advised each to mark well his or her own. All then returned to the garden, where a feast of milk-soup with eggs and egg-cakes had been prepared.

Part III

Afterward they went back to the wood, and found to their great joy in each nest five beautiful colored eggs, and on one of these a short rhyme was written.

The surprise and delight of the little ones when they discovered a nest of the gaily colored treasures, was very great, and one of them exclaimed:

"How wonderful the hens must be that can lay such pretty eggs! How I should like to see them!"

"Oh! No hens could lay such beautiful eggs," answered a little girl. "I think it must have been the little hare that sprang out of the juniper bush when I wanted to build my nest there."

Then all the children laughed together, and said, "The hares lay the colored eggs. Yes, yes! The dear little hares lay the beautiful eggs!" And they kept repeating it till they began really to believe it.

Not long afterward the war ended, and Duke Arno von Lindenburg took his wife and children back to their own palace; but, before leaving, the Duchess set apart a sum of money to be expended in giving the village children every Easter a feast of eggs. She instituted the custom also in her own duchy, and by degrees it spread over the whole country, the eggs being considered a symbol of redemption or deliverance from sin.

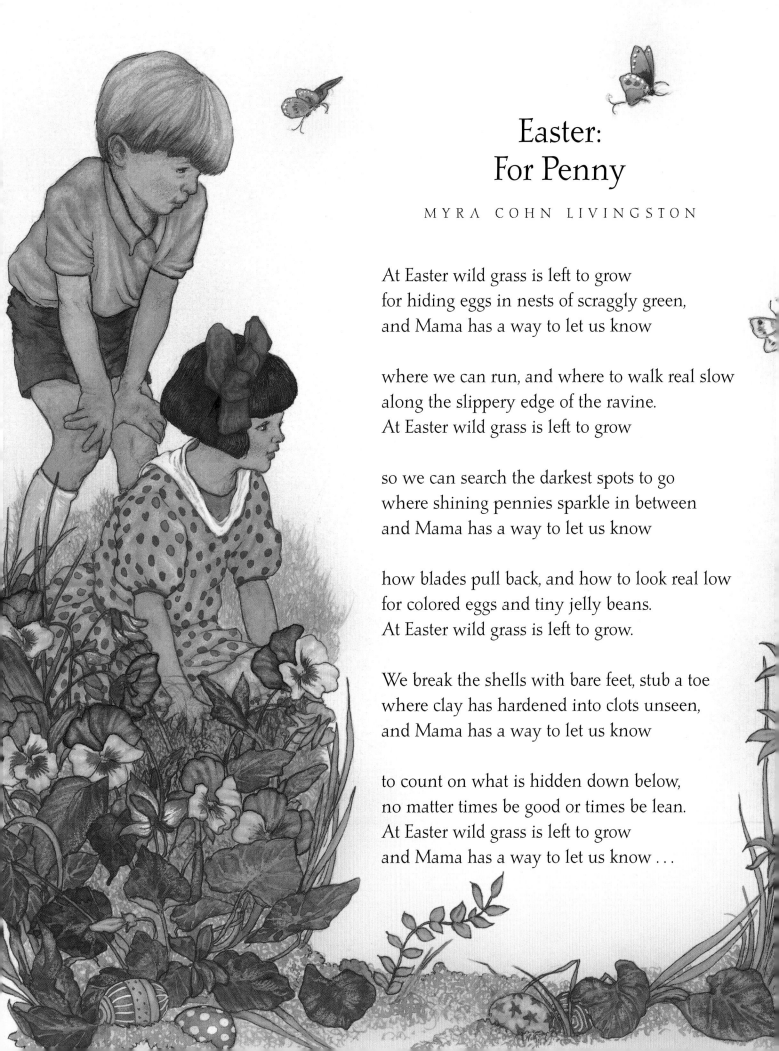

Easter:
For Penny

MYRA COHN LIVINGSTON

At Easter wild grass is left to grow
for hiding eggs in nests of scraggly green,
and Mama has a way to let us know

where we can run, and where to walk real slow
along the slippery edge of the ravine.
At Easter wild grass is left to grow

so we can search the darkest spots to go
where shining pennies sparkle in between
and Mama has a way to let us know

how blades pull back, and how to look real low
for colored eggs and tiny jelly beans.
At Easter wild grass is left to grow.

We break the shells with bare feet, stub a toe
where clay has hardened into clots unseen,
and Mama has a way to let us know

to count on what is hidden down below,
no matter times be good or times be lean.
At Easter wild grass is left to grow
and Mama has a way to let us know . . .

Bramble and Buckwheat

ETHEL POCHOCKI

One day early in spring a mother rabbit out searching for dandelion greens for supper heard a pitiful mewing in a blackberry briar. Nothing with such a tiny voice could be of harm, she thought, so she went to take a look. There, crying as if his heart would break, eyes wide and frightened, sat a mackerel tabby kitten, just about the same age as her own babies.

Without any hesitation, she hopped over to the kitten and pulled it out from under the thorny vines. "There, there," she soothed, "don't you cry. You'll come home with me and be all snug and cozy with lots of brothers and sisters."

She carried the kitten home in her teeth and went directly into the burrow to the nest lined with her fur that held six baby rabbits. "Meet your new brothers and sisters, little one!"

The mother rabbit named the kitten Bramble, and he joined the rabbit family and grew fat and frisky. They played games together, sat in the sun after they ate, and groomed themselves by licking their paws and washing their faces and ears. They chased ladybugs and tree frogs and played hide-and-seek with the little mice who skittered through the leftover dried leaves.

Bramble's special friend was Buckwheat, the largest and strongest of the rabbits. They would go off together exploring or flying kites or gathering wildflowers for the mother rabbit to identify. As the days passed, Bramble began to notice small differences between him and his friend. The ears, for one thing. Buckwheat's stood straight up, stiff and alert, while Bramble's were small and round and had little tufts of fur coming out of them.

Bramble's fur rippled in black and brown stripes, while Buckwheat's was a solid, soft reddish-brown. Bramble's tail was long and thin and Buckwheat's was a short puff of white. One's eyes were jet black and the other's were golden green. Buckwheat could thump on the ground with his strong hind feet to warn of danger, and Bramble couldn't, but he could climb a tree when danger came.

One day Bramble asked the mother rabbit about these things, and she said gently, "Why, Bramble, this is only natural. You're not a rabbit, you know, you're a cat." And she told him the story of how she had found him.

Bramble was quite upset. He didn't want to be a cat. His brothers and sisters had told him about the mean things cats did. They even caught rabbits.

"No," he said to the mother rabbit, "I am not a cat and I refuse to be one. I am a rabbit and I always will be, and that is that."

She smiled a bit sadly, since she knew that someday the stubborn little kitten would grow up to be a cat who caught mice and wouldn't think of playing with them as friends.

All the while Bramble was denying that he was a cat, spring was blossoming into Easter. The violets popped out, the streams thawed and ran merrily free, and the rabbit family ate asparagus every night.

This year Buckwheat had been given the honor of being the Easter Rabbit because of his intelligence, swiftness, and quick wits. He and his helpers would deliver the special eggs that mark the return of green life to earth and celebrate the time when everything is made new.

Some say these were magical eggs, and perhaps they were. For certain, they were beautiful. They were decorated by Great-Grandmother Rabbit, who lived not in an ordinary burrow but in a many-roomed house at the bottom of an oak tree. There she had space to spread out her pots of paint and brushes and work undisturbed.

Great-Grandmother, whose ancestors came from Lithuania, had been taught as a young rabbit how to paint perfect pictures. Now, on dozens of eggshells, she created scenes of lambs and golden crosses and roses and carrots, and, always, she hid a tiny rabbit among them.

By Easter Sunday, all was ready. The willow baskets woven by the mother rabbit were lined with watercress from the stream, decorated with yellow violets, and filled with the delicate painted eggs. Bramble and Buckwheat and the other rabbits could hardly wait for the moon to rise so they could be on their way.

Beneath their excitement, though, they were nervous and a little afraid, for they rarely went out alone at night. The mother rabbit knew the dangers all too well, but she hid her fear and waved them good-bye. "Be careful, my dears, go on your way with courage. Remember, you are spreading joy!" And she asked the angels to watch over them.

The moon was high as Bramble and the six rabbits hopped and skipped and leaped. They relished being out at night on an adventure and doing a good deed at the same time. How silly they had been to be afraid!

Bramble led the way proudly, head up, tail into the wind. Then, right behind, came Buckwheat, basket on his arm. He was followed by his brothers and sisters, with their baskets. The deep rich colors of the eggs glistened in the moonlight.

The group went first to the homes of the mouse, squirrel, and

chipmunk families, tucking the baskets into the grass by their nests and trees. They left none in the birds' nests, because one year when they did, a poor mother bird had sat on hers for weeks, waiting for it to hatch.

Then the group went to the cottages of the humans who lived by the edge of the woods—a shepherd and his family, a young widow who sold herbs, a cranky old man who had been known to smile only once, and then in his youth.

"Watch out for the old man," whispered Buckwheat. "He has a temper." He left the basket on the porch, silently as possible. Bramble, who wanted to see a cranky old man, lingered behind to peer into the window. The old man was flat on his back in bed, his mouth open, and was snoring loudly. Curled up close to him was a large mackerel tabby, almost but not quite asleep.

She opened her eyes and stared directly at the window and Bramble. Bramble's eyes met hers and he had a sudden memory of another tabby who had loved him. For a moment, neither moved. Then the other cat blinked; her gaze softened and was not unfriendly. Bramble felt a tinge of joyful kinship.

"Come on, Bramble," whispered Buckwheat, who was getting anxious, "it's almost dawn and we still have the farmer's basket to deliver." Bramble sighed and left a smudge with his nose on the window and joined the others in their mad, happy dash across the meadow to the farm.

The farmer and his wife had kindly shared their summer garden with the rabbits, so of course they must be remembered, but they kept a large dog named Bruno, who terrified the rabbits. Once he had escaped his yard and torn off into the woods. The rabbits had never seen such a huge beast and they panicked, streaking across one another's paths, bumping into one another on their way to their burrows. Now they were in *his* territory.

Buckwheat quietly hopped up the steps with Bramble, while the others waited at the bottom. Buckwheat had just put the basket down when Bramble suddenly let out a loud sneeze. It was not a dainty, whispery sneeze, but a snort loud enough to be a human's.

The sneeze blasted Bruno out of a pleasant dream and he staggered to his feet, ready to take on any intruders. Who would dare come into his yard? Did they mean any harm to the master? He would soon take care of them!

Bruno growled and galloped toward them. The rabbits froze in fear. They could not breathe, twitch, or blink their staring eyes. Bramble alone sprang into action. He ran toward Bruno as if he had just found a long-lost friend. Bruno stopped to sniff at this bold creature and saw it was a cat. He did not like cats. The big ones in the house teased him and jumped on his tail and he knew they mocked him behind his back. No, another cat would not do.

He grabbed Bramble in his mouth and dangled the kitten by his neck. "Run, all of you, run," Bramble yowled to the rabbits. "I can take care of myself."

With that, he swatted at Bruno's ear with one paw and nicked it, and with the other, he made a deep trail across Bruno's nose. The dog yelped and dropped Bramble, who scrambled to his feet and ran around Bruno in circles. Finally, when the dog seemed ready to drop with dizziness, Bramble climbed up an apple tree and taunted Bruno to come catch him. By then, all the rabbits had fled. The dog sat gloomily at the foot of the tree for a while, then lurched toward his doghouse, whimpering softly.

When the farmer opened the door and saw the Easter basket, he smiled and said, "What do you know—he's come again! Bruno, were you barking at the Easter Rabbit? Shame on you, you should know better." Bruno sighed, lay down, closed his eyes, and hoped the rest of the day would be better.

Bramble got back to the burrow shortly after the rabbits and there were great whoops of joy and cries of relief. The mother rabbit wiped her eyes, for she knew the strength of Bruno and the littleness of Bramble, and said it was a miracle. Then they all sat down to a special breakfast of parsnip-and-acorn stew and currant buns. But first the mother rabbit said grace and gave thanks that all had come home safely. She said none of her children could have challenged Bruno as cleverly as Bramble and enabled them to escape.

"You see, Bramble," she said, "there are good things about being a cat, even if you can't thump or hop or build a burrow."

Bramble was so pleased with himself, he decided to do something catlike after breakfast and go for a leisurely walk.

"Now don't be gone too long," warned the mother rabbit. "We've had enough excitement already. And later we'll go down and greet the ducks. They've just arrived."

"I won't go too far," promised Bramble. "I just thought I'd go visit the cranky old man. And his cat."

Easter Day

ANONYMOUS

Thirty days hath September,
        Every person can remember;
But to know when Easter'll come
        Puzzles even scholars, some.

When March the twenty-first is past
        Just watch the silvery moon,
And when you see it full and round,
        Know Easter'll be here soon.

After the moon has reached its full,
        Then Easter will be here,
On the very Sunday after
        In each and every year.

And if it hap on Sunday
        The moon should reach its height,
The Sunday following this event
        Will be the Easter bright.

A Time of Love

The Gospel According to St. John
19:1–2, 17–18, 38–42, 20:1–31

KING JAMES VERSION

Then Pilate therefore took Jesus, and scourged him. And the soldiers platted a crown of thorns, and put it on his head, and they put on him a purple robe, and he bearing his cross went forth into a place called the place of a skull, which is called in the Hebrew Golgotha: where they crucified him, and two other with him, on either side one, and Jesus in the midst.

And after this Joseph of Arimathaea, being a disciple of Jesus, but secretly for fear of the Jews, besought Pilate that he might take away the body of Jesus: and Pilate gave him leave. He came therefore, and took the body of Jesus. And there came also Nicodemus, which at the first came to Jesus by night, and brought a mixture of myrrh and aloes, about an hundred pound weight. Then took they the body of Jesus, and wound it in linen clothes with the spices, as the manner of the Jews is to bury. Now in the place where he was crucified there was a garden; and in the garden a new sepulchre, wherein was never man yet laid. There laid they Jesus therefore because of the Jews' preparation day; for the sepulchre was nigh at hand.

The first day of the week cometh Mary Magdalene early, when it was yet dark, unto the sepulchre, and seeth the stone taken away from the sepulchre. Then she runneth, and cometh to Simon Peter, and to the other disciple, whom Jesus loved, and saith unto them, They have taken away the Lord out of the sepulchre, and we know not where they have laid him. Peter therefore went forth, and that other disciple, and came to the sepulchre. So they ran both together: and the other disciple did outrun Peter, and came first to the sepulchre. And he stooping down, and looking in, saw the linen clothes lying; yet went he not in. Then cometh Simon Peter following him, and went into the sepulchre, and seeth the linen clothes lie, And the napkin, that was about his head, not lying with the linen clothes, but wrapped together in a place by itself. Then went in also that other disciple, which came first to the sepulchre, and he saw, and believed. For as yet they knew not the scripture, that he must rise again from the dead. Then the disciples went away again unto their own home. But Mary stood without at the sepulchre weeping: and as she wept, she stooped down, and looked into the sepulchre, and seeth two angels in white sitting, the one at the head, and the other at the feet, where the body of Jesus had lain. And they say unto her, Woman, why weepest thou? She saith unto them, Because they have taken away my Lord, and I know not where they have laid him. And when she had thus said, she turned herself back, and saw Jesus standing, and knew not that it was Jesus.

Jesus saith unto her, Woman, why weepest thou? whom seekest thou? She, supposing him to be the gardener, saith unto him, Sir, if thou have borne him hence, tell me where thou hast laid him, and I will take him away. Jesus saith unto her, Mary. She turned herself, and saith unto him, Rabboni; which is to say, Master. Jesus saith unto her, Touch me not; for I am not yet ascended to my Father: but go to my brethren, and say unto them, I ascend unto my Father, and your Father; and to my God, and your God.

Mary Magdalene came and told the disciples that she had seen the Lord, and that he had spoken these things unto her. Then the same day at evening, being the first day of the week, when the doors were shut where the disciples were assembled for fear of the Jews, came Jesus and stood in the midst, and saith unto them, Peace be unto you. And when he had so said, he shewd unto them his hands and his side. Then were the disciples glad, when they saw the Lord. Then said Jesus to them again, Peace be unto you: as my Father hath sent me, even so send I you. And when he had said this, he breathed on them, and saith unto them, Receive ye the Holy Ghost: Whose soever sins ye remit, they are remitted unto them; and whose soever sins ye retain, they are retained.

But Thomas, one of the twelve, called Didymus, was not with them when Jesus came. The other disciples therefore said unto him, We have seen the Lord. But he said unto them, Except I shall see in his hands the print of the nails, and put my finger into the print of the nails, and thrust my hand into his side, I will not believe. And after eight days again his disciples were within, and Thomas with them: then came Jesus, the doors being shut, and stood in the midst, and said, Peace be unto you. Then saith he to Thomas, reach hither thy finger, and behold my hands; and reach hither thy hand, and thrust it into my side: and be not faithless, but believing. And Thomas answered and said unto him, My Lord and my God. Jesus saith unto him, Thomas, because thou hast seen me, thou hast believed: blessed are they that have not seen, and yet have believed. And many other signs truly did Jesus in the presence of his disciples, which are not written in this book: But these are written, that ye might believe that Jesus is the Christ, the Son of God; and that believing ye might have life through his name.

An Easter Carol

CHRISTINA GEORGINA ROSSETTI

Spring bursts to-day,
For Christ is risen and all the earth's at play.

Flash forth, thou Sun,
The rain is over and gone, its work is done.

Winter is past,
Sweet Spring is come at last, is come at last.

Bud, Fig and Vine,
Bud, Olive, fat with fruit and oil and wine.

Break forth this morn
In roses, thou but yesterday a thorn.

Uplift thy head,
O pure white Lily through the Winter dead.

Beside your dams
Leap and rejoice, you merry-making Lambs.

All Herds and Flocks
Rejoice, all Beasts of thickets and of rocks.

Sing, Creatures, sing,
Angels and Men and Birds and everything.

All notes of Doves
Fill all our world: this is the time of loves.

The White Blackbird

PADRAIC COLUM

O h, no, it cannot be," said all the creatures of the farmyard when the little wren told them what she had seen.

"Yes, yes, yes," said the little wren excitedly. "I flew and I fluttered along the hedges, and I saw it, just as I tell you."

"What did you see, oh, what did you see?" asked the foolish pigeons. They came to where the cock with the hens was standing, and they stretched out their necks to hear what was being said.

"Something too terrible to talk to foolish creatures about," said the cock as he went gloomily away.

"Too terrible, too terrible," said the robin redbreast mournfully, as she went hopping under the hedge.

Inside the house the Boy was standing, and he was looking into a cage. Within that cage was a bird he had caught. It was the most wonderful of all birds, for it was a white Blackbird. Now you might live a whole lifetime and never once see a white Blackbird. But this Boy had not only seen a white Blackbird—he had caught one.

He had put the white Blackbird into a cage, and he was going to keep it forever. He was a lonely Boy, this Boy who had caught the white Blackbird. His father he had never known. His mother was dead. He lived in the house of his grandmother, his mother's mother.

His father had once lived here, but that was at a time that the Boy had no remembrance of. Then, his mother being dead, his father and his grandmother had quarreled, and after that his father went away and was never heard of afterward. The Boy had no one to take him by the hand as other boys had. He used to tell his grandmother about seeing boys walking with their fathers, the boys holding their fathers' hands. But he had given up telling her about such sights, for she looked lonely when he spoke of them.

Now the Boy had a bird for his very own. That was a joy to him. The night before the Peep-show Man had been in the house. He came out carrying a lantern. He held the lantern into a bush. The light came upon a bird that was resting there. Dazzled by the light, the bird did not move, and the Peep-show Man put his hand upon the bird, caught it, and gave it to the Boy to keep. This was the white Blackbird.

The Boy put the bird into an empty cage. Now that he had something of his own, he would not be lonely nor sorry for himself when he saw such and such a boy walking with his father on the Easter Sunday that was coming. All day he watched the strange white bird. And that night as he sat by the fire his eyes were upon the cage, and he watched the stirring of the white Blackbird within.

The robin redbreast that in the winter goes along under the hedge, and the little wren that flies along the top of the hedge, were talking to each other. "Always, on Easter Sunday," said the wren, "I sing my first song of the year. My first song is for the risen Lord." "And mine, too," said the robin redbreast. "But now we will not know that it is Easter Morning and that it is time to sing for the risen Lord. For the white Blackbird always showed itself to us in times before, and when it showed itself we knew it was Easter indeed."

"Oh, now we know what has happened," said the foolish pigeons. "The Boy has caught the white Blackbird that used to appear just before the sun was up every Easter Morning. He has brought the white Blackbird into the house and he has put it into a cage. It will not be able to show itself. Dear, dear, dear! We are truly sorry."

"The songs that the robin and the wren sing are not so very important," said the cock. "But think of the proclamation that I have made every Easter Morning. *Mok an o-ee Slaun,* 'The Son of the Virgin is safe.' I made it when the white Blackbird showed himself. Now men will not know that they may be rejoiceful."

"I—" said the wren, looking around very bravely.

"The world will be the worse for not hearing my tidings," said the cock.

"I—" said the wren again.

"The wren is trying to say something, and no one will listen to her," said robin redbreast.

"Oh, by all means let the wren keep on talking," said the cock, and he went away.

"Tell us, tell us," said the pigeons.

"I," said the little wren, "will try to set the white Blackbird free."

"How, how?" asked the foolish pigeons.

"I might fly into the house when no one is watching," said the wren. "I can really slip into and out of places without being seen. I might manage to open the door of the cage that the white Blackbird is in."

"Oh, it is terrible in the house," said the foolish pigeons; "we went in once picking grains. The door was closed on us. It was dark in there. And we saw the terrible green eyes of the cat watching us. It is terrible in the house." Then the pigeons flew away.

"I should be afraid to go in," said the robin redbreast, "now that they have mentioned the eyes of the cat."

"I *am* afraid," said the little wren. "And there is no one that would miss me if anything terrible befell me. I really am so

afraid that I want to fly right away from this place."

But then, although her little heart was beating very fast, the wren flew up on the thatched porch. There was no one could see her there, so small and so brown she was. When darkness came outside she fluttered into the house. She hid in a corner of the dresser behind a little luster jug. She watched the cage that had the white Blackbird in it. She saw the door of the house closed and bolted for the night.

Oh, all in a fright and a flutter was the little brown wren as she hid in one of the houses of men. She saw the terrible cat sleeping by the hearth. She saw, when the fire burned low, how the cat rose and stretched herself and looked all around the house with her terrible eyes. The Boy and his grandmother had now gone up to bed.

The wren could still see by the light that blazed up on the hearth. The cat went up one step of the stairs, but only a step. For as the wren fluttered up and alighted on the top of the cage the cat heard the sound that she made, light and all as it was, and she turned back and looked at the cage, and the little wren knew that the cat saw her and would watch her.

There was a little catch on the door of the cage. The wren pulled at it with her beak. She said to the bird within, "O white messenger—"

"How shall I fly out of the house—tell me, tell me," said the white Blackbird.

"We will fly up the chimney, and away," said the little wren as she opened the door.

Before the darkness had quite gone a man came along the road that went by that house. He had on the clothes of a soldier. He stood and looked at the house as he came before it. His little boy was there. But he would not stay to see him. The memory of the quarrel that he had had with the woman who lived there, the boy's grandmother, came over him. His heart was made bitter by that memory, and he would not cross her threshold.

It was near daylight now. Out of the hedge came a thin, little song. It was the song of the wren, he knew, and he smiled as he listened to it. He heard another song, a song with joyous notes in it, the first song that the robin sings from the hedge tops. All the times before she has been going under the hedges without a song.

And then he heard the cock crow. Loudly, loudly, the cock cried *"Mok an o-ee Slaun, mok an o-ee Slaun,"* and the man remembered that this was Easter Morning. He did not go on now. He waited, and he stood looking at the house.

And then, upon the thatch of the porch he saw a strange bird—a strange, white bird. The man could not go on now. Only once in a lifetime might one see a white Blackbird. And this was the second time he had seen one. Once before, and on an Easter Morning too, he had seen a white Blackbird. He had come to this house. Some-one was living in it then who was dead since. The girl who be-came the mother of his boy was living here. He had come for her to this house so that they might go out together and see the sun rising on Easter Morning. And when he had come before the house he had seen a strange bird on the thatch of the porch—he had seen the white Blackbird then as he saw it now.

He did not go.

Then out of the house came a little Boy. He held an empty cage in his hand. He looked all around. He saw the white Blackbird upon the porch, and he held his hands to the bird as if trying to draw it down to him again.

The man went to the Boy. And the Boy, knowing him, caught

the hand that was held to him. The Boy drew the man within.
There was a woman at the hearth. She turned and saw the man.

"And you are safe, my daughter's comrade?" said the woman as
she drew the man to her. "And now the child will have his father
to take him by the hand this Easter."

The Boy felt that he would never again be lonely. He heard the
robin singing. He heard the wren singing. He heard the cock outside telling the world about the risen Lord. He saw the white Blackbird flying away.

Spring

GERARD MANLEY HOPKINS

Nothing is so beautiful as spring—
    When weeds, in wheels, shoot long and lovely and lush;
    Thrush's eggs look little low heavens, and thrush
Through the echoing timber does so rinse and wring
The ear, it strikes like lightnings to hear him sing;

The glassy peartree leaves and blooms, they brush
    The descending blue; that blue is all in a rush
With richness; the racing lambs too have fair their fling.

What is all this juice and all this joy?
    A strain of the earth's sweet being in the beginning
In Eden garden—Have, get, before it cloy,
    Before it cloud, Christ, lord, and sour with sinning,
Innocent mind and Mayday in girl and boy,
    Most, O maid's child, thy choice and worthy the winning.

The Easter Flower

CLAUDE McKAY

Far from this foreign Easter damp and chilly
    My soul steals to a pear-shaped plot of ground
Where gleamed the lilac-tinted Easter Lily
    Soft-scented in the air for yards around;

Alone, without a hint of guardian leaf!
    Just like a fragile bell of silver rime,
It burst the tomb for freedom sweet and brief
    In the young pregnant year at Eastertime;

And many thought it was a sacred sign,
    And some called it the resurrection flower;
And I, in wonder, worshiped at its shrine,
    Yielding my heart unto its perfumed power.

The Rat-Catcher's Daughter

LAURENCE HOUSMAN

Once upon a time there lived an old rat-catcher who had a daughter, the most beautiful girl that had ever been born. Their home was a dirty little cabin; but they were not so poor as they seemed, for every night the rat-catcher took the rats he had cleared out of one house and let them go at the door of another, so that on the morrow he might be sure of a fresh job.

His rats got quite to know him and would run to him when he called; people thought him the most wonderful rat-catcher and could not make out how it was that a rat remained within reach of his operations.

Now anyone can see that a man who practiced so cunning a roguery was greedy beyond the intentions of Providence. Every day, as he watched his daughter's beauty increase, his thoughts were: "When will she be able to pay me back for all the expense she has been to me?" He would have grudged her the very food she ate, if it had not been necessary to keep her in the good looks, which were some day to bring him his fortune. For he was greedier than any gnome after gold.

Now all good gnomes have this about them: they love whatever is beautiful and hate to see harm happen to it. A gnome who lived far away underground below where stood the rat-catcher's house, said to his fellows: "Up yonder is a man who has a daughter; so greedy is he, he would sell her to the first comer who gave him gold enough! I am going up to look after her."

So one night, when the rat-catcher set a trap, the gnome went and got himself caught in it. There in the morning, when the rat-catcher came, he found a funny little fellow, all bright and golden, wriggling and beating to be free.

"I can't get out!" cried the little gnome. "Let me go!"

The rat-catcher screwed up his mouth to look virtuous. "If I let you out, what will you give me?"

"A sack full of gold," answered the gnome, "just as heavy as myself—not a pennyweight less!"

"Not enough!" said the rat-catcher. "Guess again!"

"As heavy as you are!" cried the gnome, beginning to plead in a thin, whining tone.

"I'm a poor man," said the rat-catcher; "a poor man mayn't afford to be generous!"

"What is it you want of me?" cried the gnome.

"If I let you go," said the rat-catcher, "you must make me the

richest man in the world!" Then he thought of his daughter: "Also you must make the king's son marry my daughter; then I will let you go."

The gnome laughed to himself to see how the trapper was being trapped in his own avarice as, with the most melancholy air, he answered: "I can make you the richest man in the world; but I know of no way of making the king's son marry your daughter, except one."

"What way?" asked the rat-catcher.

"Why," answered the gnome, "for three years your daughter must come and live with me underground, and by the end of the third year her skin will be changed into pure gold like ours. And do you know any king's son who would refuse to marry a beautiful maiden who was pure gold from the sole of her foot to the crown of her head?"

The rat-catcher had so greedy an inside that he could not believe in any king's son refusing to marry a maiden of pure gold. So he clapped hands on the bargain and let the gnome go.
The gnome went down into the ground and fetched up sacks and sacks of gold, until he had made the rat-catcher the richest man in the world. Then the father called his daughter, whose name was Jasomé, and bade her follow the gnome down into the heart of the earth.

It was all in vain that Jasomé begged and implored; the rat-catcher was bent on having her married to the king's son. So he pushed, and the gnome pulled, and down she went; and the earth closed after her.

The gnome brought her down to his home under the hill upon which stood the town. Everywhere round her were gold and precious stones; the very air was full of gold dust, so that when she remained still it settled on her hands and her hair, and a soft golden down began to show itself over her skin. So there in the house of the gnome sat Jasomé and cried; and, far away overhead, she heard the days come and go by the sound of people walking and the rolling of wheels.

The gnome was very kind to her; nothing did he spare of underground commodities that might afford her pleasure. He taught her the legends of all the heroes that have gone down into earth and been forgotten, and the lost songs of the old poets, and the buried languages that once gave wisdom to the world: down there all these things are remembered.

She became the most curiously accomplished and wise maiden that ever was hidden from the light of day. "I have to train you," said the gnome, "to be fit for a king's bride!" But Jasomé, though she thanked him, only cried to be let out.

In front of the rat-catcher's house rose a little spring of salt water with gold dust in it, that gilded the basin where it sprang. When he saw it, he began rubbing his hands with delight, for he guessed well enough that his daughter's tears had made it; and the dust in it told him how surely now she was being turned into gold.

And now the rat-catcher was the richest man in the world: all his traps were made of gold, and when he went rat-hunting he rode in a gilded coach drawn by twelve hundred of the finest and largest rats. This was for an advertisement of the business. He now caught rats for the fun of it and the show of it, but also to get money by it; for, though he was so rich, ratting and money-grubbing had become a second nature to him; unless he were at one or the other, he could not be happy.

Far below, in the house of the gnome, Jasomé sat and cried.

When the sound of the great bells ringing for Easter came down to her, the gnome said: "Today I cannot bind you; it is the great rising day for all Christians. If you wish, you may go up and ask your father now to release you."

So Jasomé kissed the gnome and went up the track of her own tears that brought her to her father's door. When she came to the light of day, she felt quite blind; a soft yellow tint was all over her, and already her hair was quite golden.

The rat-catcher was furious when he saw her coming back before her time. "Oh, father," she cried, "let me come back for a little while to play in the sun!" But her father, fearing lest the gilding of her complexion should be spoiled, drove her back into the earth and trampled it down over her head.

The gnome seemed quite sorry for her when she returned; but already, he said, a year was gone—and what were three years when a king's son would be the reward?

At the next Easter he let her go again; and now she looked quite golden, except for her eyes and her white teeth and the nails on her pretty little fingers and toes. But again her father drove her back into the ground and put a heavy stone slab over the spot to make sure of her.

At last the third Easter came, and she was all gold.

She kissed the gnome many times and was almost sorry to leave him, for he had been very kind to her. And now he told her about her father catching him in the trap, and robbing him of his gold by a hard bargain, and of his being forced to take her down to live with him till she was turned into gold, so that she might marry the king's son. "For now," said he, "you are so compounded of gold that only the gnomes could rub it off you."

So this time, when Jasomé came up once more to the light of day, she did not go back again to her cruel father but went and sat by the roadside and played with the sunbeams and wondered when the king's son would come and marry her.

And as she sat there all the country people who passed by stopped and mocked her; and boys came and threw mud at her because she was all gold from head to foot—an object, to be sure, for all simple folk to laugh at. So presently, instead of hoping, she fell to despair and sat weeping with her face hidden in her hands.

Before long the king's son came down that road and saw something shining like sunlight on a pond; but when he came near, he found a lovely maiden of pure gold lying in a pool of her own tears with her face hidden in her hair.

Now the king's son, unlike the country folk, knew the value of gold; but he was grieved at heart for a maiden so stained all over with it, and more, when he beheld how she wept. So he went to lift her up; and there, surely, he saw the most beautiful face he could ever have dreamed of. But, alas! So discolored—even her eyes, and her lips, and the very tears she shed were the color of gold! When he could bring her to speak, she told him how, because she was all gold, all the people mocked at her and boys threw mud at her; and she had nowhere to go, unless it were back to the kind gnome who lived underground, out of sight of the sweet sun.

So the prince said, "Come with me, and I will take you to my father's palace, and there nobody shall mock you, but you shall sit all your days in the sunshine and be happy."

And as they went, more and more he wondered at her great beauty—so spoiled that he could not look at her without grief—and was taken with increasing wonder at the beautiful wisdom stored in her golden mind; for she told him the tales of the heroes, which she had learned from the gnome, and of buried cities; also the songs of old poets that have been forgotten; and her voice, like the rest of her, was golden.

The prince said to himself, "I shut my eyes and am ready to die loving her; yet, when I open them, she is but a talking statue!"

One day he said to her, "Under all this disguise you must be the most beautiful thing upon earth! Already to me you are the dearest!" and he sighed, for he knew that a king's son might not marry a figure of gold.

Now one day after this, as Jasomé sat alone in the sunshine and cried, the little old gnome stood before her and said, "Well, Jasomé, have you married the king's son?"

"Alas!" cried Jasomé. "You have so changed me: I am no longer human! Yet he loves me, and, but for that, he would marry me."

"Dear me!" said the gnome. "If that is all, I can take the gold off of you again: why, I said so!"

Jasomé entreated him, by all his former kindness, to do so for her now.

"Yes," said the gnome, "but a bargain is a bargain. Now is the time for me to get back my bags of gold. Do you go to your father and let him know that the king's son is willing to marry you if he restores to me my treasure that he took from me; for that is what it comes to."

Up jumped Jasomé and ran to the rat-catcher's house. "Oh, father," she cried, "now you can undo all your cruelty to me; for now, if you will give back the gnome his gold, he will give my own face back to me, and I shall marry the king's son!"

But the rat-catcher was filled with admiration at the sight of her and would not believe a word she said. "I have given you your dowry," he answered; "three years I had to do without you to get it. Take it away, and get married, and leave me the peace and plenty I have so hardly earned!"

Jasomé went back and told the gnome. "Really," said he, "I must show this rat-catcher that there are other sorts of traps and that it isn't only rats and gnomes that get caught in them! I have given him his taste of wealth; now it shall act as pickle to his poverty!"

So the next time the rat-catcher put his foot out of doors, the ground gave way under it and—snap!—the gnome had him by the leg.

"Let me go!" cried the rat-catcher; "I can't get out!"

"Can't you?" said the gnome. "If I let you out, what will you give me?"

"My daughter!" cried the rat-catcher; "my beautiful golden daughter!"

"Oh, no!" laughed the gnome. "Guess again!"

"My own weight in gold!" cried the rat-catcher, in a frenzy; but the gnome would not close the bargain till he had wrung from the rat-catcher the promise of his last penny.

So the gnome carried away all the sacks of gold before the rat-catcher's eyes; and when he had them safe underground, then at last he let the old man go. Then he called Jasomé to follow him, and she went down willingly into the black earth.

For a whole year the gnome rubbed and scrubbed and tubbed her to get the gold out of her composition; and when it was done, she was the most shiningly beautiful thing you ever set eyes on.

When she got back to the palace, she found her dear prince pining for love of her, and wondering when she would return. So they were married the very next day; and the rat-catcher came to look on at the wedding.

He grumbled because he was in rags and because he was poor; he wept that he had been robbed of his money and his daughter. But gnomes and daughters, he said, were in one and the same box; such ingratitude as theirs no one could beat.

The Lamb

WILLIAM BLAKE

Little Lamb, who made thee?
  Dost thou know who made thee?
Gave thee life, and bid thee feed,
By the stream and o'er the mead;
Gave thee clothing of delight,
Softest clothing, woolly, bright;
Gave thee such a tender voice,
Making all the vales rejoice?
  Little Lamb, who made thee?
  Dost thou know who made thee?

  Little Lamb, I'll tell thee,
  Little Lamb, I'll tell thee:
He is called by thy name,
For He calls Himself a Lamb.
He is meek, and He is mild;
He became a little child.
I a child, and thou a lamb,
We are called by His name.
  Little Lamb, God bless thee!
  Little Lamb, God bless thee!

The Sun Comes Dancing

ELIZABETH COATSWORTH

On Easter morn,
On Easter morn,
The sun comes dancing up the sky.

His light leaps up;
It shakes and swings,
Bewildering the dazzled eye.

On Easter morn
All earth is glad;
The waves rejoice in the bright sea.

Be still and listen
To your heart,
And hear it beating merrily!

j808.803 Michael Hague's
Michael   family Easter
          treasury.

$19.95   Grades 3-4

DATE			

BAKER & TAYLOR